Contents

Introduction

The mathematical concept of a *path* in a network is powerful in enabling a wide range of problems to be represented and solved. Typical examples include finding an appropriate route through a road system, or scheduling a building project by ordering related activities as a path in time from the commencement to the completion of the project.

Often we want to choose the 'best', or 'optimal', path. Finding paths involves all four types of combinatorial problem discussed in the *Introduction* unit.

Existence problem: does there exist a path between two given vertices?

Construction problem: can we construct a path?

Enumeration problem: how many paths are there?
can we list them all?

Optimization problem: can we find the 'best' paths available?

Situations in which we wish to find optimal paths are often naturally modelled using networks. Usually the arc appropriately models the transition from one state or position to another, and the optimization problem is in terms of weights attached to the arcs and/or the vertices (capacities, lengths, costs, times). Network theory enables us to define *optimal* for particular situations, and gives methods for finding the optimal paths. These methods are often expressed as algorithms which find the desired optimal paths by construction.

In this unit we show how various situations can be modelled by networks, and we present several algorithms for finding different types of optimal path.

In Section 1, *Algorithms using adjacency matrices*, we study walks in a digraph, and show that we can establish their existence by using the adjacency matrix of the digraph. We then consider walks with special properties, and show how to find Eulerian trails and Hamiltonian cycles in a digraph by working directly with the adjacency matrix.

In Section 2, *Optimal path algorithms*, we describe two algorithms: a *shortest path* algorithm and a *longest path* algorithm. Finding the shortest path has applications in areas such as road, rail and air transport planning. However, the shortest path problem can appear in many other guises, such as telecommunications and the design of complex machines.

In Section 3, *Critical path analysis*, we consider the problem of finding optimal paths in *activity networks*. These are networks representing the various stages in the completion of a project involving a number of related activities. An optimal path represents an optimum *schedule* for the project. Within such networks, some activities are *critical* in the sense that any delay in completing them delays the completion of the whole project. Critical path analysis identifies these activities and finds paths with the minimum completion time for the project, given a sufficient number of workers, thus establishing the optimum time that can be achieved in the given circumstances.

In Section 4, *Scheduling*, we discuss the related problem of finding the optimum schedule for the activities of a project when the number of workers available is restricted. In this type of problem, the critical path cannot usually be achieved; however, it is important to minimize the completion time.

In practical situations involving the organization of projects, the optimum solution may not be the completion of the project in the minimum time, but the completion of the project within an acceptable time with the minimum number of workers or minimum resources. For example, we may wish to determine how many workers or machines are needed to complete an assembly task within a given number of days. This type of problem can be represented as a combinatorial *packing problem*, and is discussed briefly in Section 5, *Bin packing*.

1 Algorithms using adjacency matrices

This section requires you to carry out matrix multiplication. If you are not familiar with matrix manipulations or need to revise them, use the computer activity on **Matrix manipulation** in the *Computer Activities Booklet*.

One of the first questions we may ask about a graph or digraph is: are two given vertices connected by a path? This is an *existence* problem. Related to this is the corresponding *enumeration* problem: how many walks or paths are there connecting any given pair of vertices? In particular, we may be interested in finding all the paths with some particular property, such as Eulerian trails or Hamiltonian cycles. In this section we show how we can solve these problems by using the adjacency matrix of the graph or digraph. As this is a *Networks* unit, we concentrate on digraphs; however, several of our results have analogues for graphs.

Adjacency matrices were defined in *Graphs 1*, Section 4.1.

1.1 Walks in digraphs

We begin by considering *walks* rather than *paths*; that is, we do not require all the vertices or all the arcs to be different.

Consider the following digraph and table.

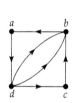

	a	b	c	d
a	0	0	0	1
b	1	0	0	0
c	0	1	0	0
d	0	2	1	0

The table shows the number of walks of length 1 between each pair of vertices, for example:

the number of walks of length 1 from a to c is **0**,

so **0** appears in row 1 column 3;

the number of walks of length 1 from b to a is **1**,

so **1** appears in row 2 and column 1;

the number of walks of length 1 from d to b is **2**,

so **2** appears in row 4 column 2.

Now a walk of length 1 is an arc, so the table above is the *adjacency matrix* **A** of the digraph (shown in the margin).

Next, we consider walks of lengths 2 and 3. For example, there are two different walks of length 2 from a to b, since there is one arc from a to d and there are two arcs from d to b. Similarly, there are two different walks of length 3 from d to d, since there are two arcs from d to b, and one walk of length 2 from b to d, namely, bad.

$$\begin{bmatrix} 0 & 0 & 0 & 1 \\ 1 & 0 & 0 & 0 \\ 0 & 1 & 0 & 0 \\ 0 & 2 & 1 & 0 \end{bmatrix}$$
adjacency matrix **A**

Problem 1.1

(a) Complete the following tables for the numbers of walks of lengths 2 and 3 in the above digraph.

	a	b	c	d
a	2			
b			1	
c				
d				

numbers of walks of length 2

	a	b	c	d
a				
b				
c				
d			2	

numbers of walks of length 3

(b) Find the matrix products $\mathbf{A}^2$ and $\mathbf{A}^3$, where $\mathbf{A}$ is the adjacency matrix of the above digraph.

(c) Comment on your results.

The solution to the above problem illustrates the following theorem.

Theorem 1.1

Let D be a digraph with n vertices labelled 1, 2, ..., n; let $\mathbf{A}$ be its adjacency matrix with respect to this listing of the vertices, and let k be any positive integer. Then the number of walks of length k from vertex i to vertex j is equal to the entry in row i and column j of the matrix $\mathbf{A}^k$.

$\mathbf{A}^k$ is the kth power of the matrix $\mathbf{A}$.

Proof

The proof is by mathematical induction on k, the length of the walk.

Proofs by induction are discussed in the Appendix to *Graphs 1*.

STEP 1   The result holds when $k = 1$, since the number of walks of length 1 from vertex i to vertex j is the number of arcs from vertex i to vertex j, and this is equal to the entry in row i and column j of the adjacency matrix $\mathbf{A}$.

STEP 2   We now assume that $k > 1$, and that the result holds for all positive integers less than k.

We must prove that the result holds for the positive integer k.

Consider any walk of length k from vertex i to vertex j. Such a walk consists of a walk of length $k - 1$ from vertex i to some vertex r adjacent to vertex j, followed by a walk of length 1 from vertex r to vertex j.

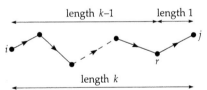

By our assumption, the number of walks of length $k - 1$ from vertex i to vertex r is the entry in row i and column r of the matrix $\mathbf{A}^{k-1}$, which we denote by $a_{ir}^{(k-1)}$. Since the number of walks of length 1 from vertex r to vertex j is a_{rj}, it follows that

the number of walks of length k from vertex i to vertex j

via vertex r (at the previous step) is $a_{ir}^{(k-1)}a_{rj}$.   (*)

We used a_{ij} to denote the element in row i and column j in a matrix $\mathbf{A}$.
We use $a_{ij}^{(k-1)}$ to denote the element in row i and column j in the matrix $\mathbf{A}^{k-1}$.

Now the total number of walks of length k from vertex i to vertex j equals

the number of such walks via vertex 1 (at the previous step)

+ the number of such walks via vertex 2 (at the previous step)

. . .

+ the number of such walks via vertex r (at the previous step)

. . .

+ the number of such walks via vertex n (at the previous step).

The Open University

MT365 Graphs, networks and design

Networks 2

Optimal paths

Study guide

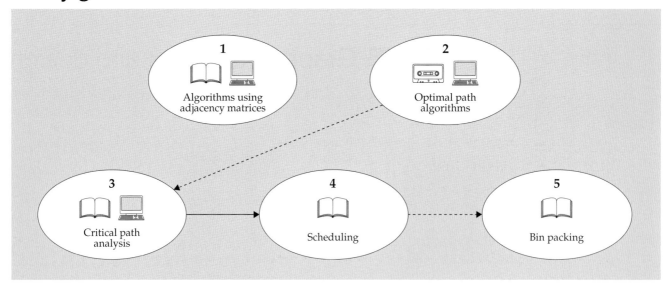

This unit introduces several algorithms, chosen to illustrate typical approaches to some standard types of problem involving some form of optimization.

The five sections are largely independent and, with the exception of Sections 3 and 4, need not be studied in numerical order.

Section 1 revises and extends ideas introduced in *Graphs 1*. It involves the calculation of sums and products of matrices; the examples chosen are very simple and do not take long to calculate directly. However, you may prefer to use the ***Matrix manipulation*** package. *If you are not familiar with matrix operations, you will need to use this package to familiarize yourself with the basic ideas before studying Section 1.* There is a computer activity designed to help you to do this in the *Computer Activities Booklet*.

Section 2 is an audio-tape section which introduces two short, but important, algorithms.

Sections 1, 2 and 3 are followed by computer activities.

The Open University, Walton Hall, Milton Keynes, MK7 6AA.

First published 1995. Reprinted 1997, 2000, 2002, 2003, 2005, 2008, 2009.

ISBN 0 7492 2226 3

1.6

By our previous result (∗), this is equal to

$$a_{i1}^{(k-1)}a_{1j} + a_{i2}^{(k-1)}a_{2j} + \cdots + a_{ir}^{(k-1)}a_{rj} + \cdots + a_{in}^{(k-1)}a_{nj}.$$

By the rules for matrix multiplication, this is the entry in row i and column j of the matrix product $\mathbf{A}^{k-1}\mathbf{A} = \mathbf{A}^k$, as required.

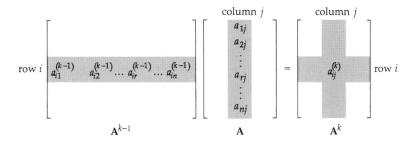

Thus, if the result holds for all positive integers less than k, then it holds for the integer k. This completes Step 2.

Therefore, by the principle of mathematical induction, the theorem is true for all integers k. ■

Problem 1.2 ────────────────────────────────

Consider the following digraph.

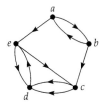

Write down the adjacency matrix $\mathbf{A}$, calculate the matrices $\mathbf{A}^2$, $\mathbf{A}^3$ and $\mathbf{A}^4$, and hence find the numbers of walks of lengths 1, 2, 3 and 4 from b to d. Is there a walk of length 1, 2, 3 or 4 from d to b?

──

Theorem 1.1 also gives us a method of determining whether a digraph is strongly connected, by working directly from its adjacency matrix.

Recall that a digraph is *strongly connected* if there is a path from vertex i to vertex j, for each pair of vertices i and j, and that a path is a walk in which all the vertices are different. For example, in the digraph considered earlier, there are four vertices, so a path has length 1, 2 or 3. We have seen that the numbers of walks (including the paths) of lengths 1, 2 and 3 between pairs of distinct vertices are given by the non-diagonal entries in the following matrices.

If there is a *walk* from vertex i to vertex j in a digraph, then there must be a *path*, so, for convenience, we consider *walks*. Proving statements about paths is much harder than proving statements about walks.

The *diagonal* entries are those on the main diagonal from top left to bottom right.

$$\mathbf{A} = \begin{bmatrix} 0 & 0 & 0 & 1 \\ 1 & 0 & 0 & 0 \\ 0 & 1 & 0 & 0 \\ 0 & 2 & 1 & 0 \end{bmatrix} \quad \mathbf{A}^2 = \begin{bmatrix} 0 & 2 & 1 & 0 \\ 0 & 0 & 0 & 1 \\ 1 & 0 & 0 & 0 \\ 2 & 1 & 0 & 0 \end{bmatrix} \quad \mathbf{A}^3 = \begin{bmatrix} 2 & 1 & 0 & 0 \\ 0 & 2 & 1 & 0 \\ 0 & 0 & 0 & 1 \\ 1 & 0 & 0 & 2 \end{bmatrix}$$

By examining these matrices, we can see that each pair of distinct vertices is indeed joined by at least one path of length 1, 2 or 3, so the digraph is strongly connected. However, we can check this more easily if we consider the matrix $\mathbf{B}$ obtained by adding the three matrices together as shown below.

$$\mathbf{B} = \mathbf{A} + \mathbf{A}^2 + \mathbf{A}^3 = \begin{bmatrix} 2 & 3 & 1 & 1 \\ 1 & 2 & 1 & 1 \\ 1 & 1 & 0 & 1 \\ 3 & 3 & 1 & 2 \end{bmatrix}$$

In the matrix $\mathbf{B}$, each entry b_{ij} is the total number of walks of lengths 1, 2 or 3 from i to j. We see that all the non-diagonal entries are positive, which means that each pair of distinct vertices is connected by a path.

$$\mathbf{B} = \mathbf{A} + \mathbf{A}^2 + \mathbf{A}^3 = \begin{bmatrix} 2 & 3 & 1 & 1 \\ 1 & 2 & 1 & 1 \\ 1 & 1 & 0 & 1 \\ 3 & 3 & 1 & 2 \end{bmatrix}$$

We generalize this result, as follows.

Theorem 1.2

Let D be a digraph with n vertices labelled 1, 2, ..., n; let $\mathbf{A}$ be its adjacency matrix with respect to this listing of the vertices, and let $\mathbf{B}$ be the matrix

$$\mathbf{B} = \mathbf{A} + \mathbf{A}^2 + \cdots + \mathbf{A}^{n-1}.$$

Then D is strongly connected if and only if each non-diagonal entry in $\mathbf{B}$ is positive; that is, $b_{ij} > 0$ whenever $i \neq j$.

Proof

(a) If each non-diagonal entry in $\mathbf{B}$ is positive; that is, $b_{ij} > 0$ whenever $i \neq j$, then $a_{ij}^{(k)} > 0$, for some $k \leq n - 1$. Therefore there is a walk of length at most $n - 1$ from vertex i to vertex j whenever $i \neq j$, and so the digraph D is strongly connected.

(b) If the digraph D is strongly connected, then there is a path from any vertex to any other. If the digraph has n vertices, then such a path must pass through at most $n - 2$ intermediate vertices, and so must have length at most $n - 1$. It follows that $a_{ij}^{(k)} > 0$ for at least one value of $k \leq n - 1$, and hence that b_{ij}, the entry in row i and column j of $\mathbf{B}$, must be positive; that is, $b_{ij} > 0$ whenever $i \neq j$. ■

Problem 1.3

Find $\mathbf{B}$ for the digraph in Problem 1.2, and hence determine whether the digraph is strongly connected.

Problem 1.4

Use Theorem 1.2 to determine whether the digraph with the following adjacency matrix is strongly connected.

$$\begin{bmatrix} 0 & 0 & 0 & 1 & 0 \\ 1 & 0 & 1 & 0 & 0 \\ 0 & 0 & 0 & 1 & 0 \\ 0 & 0 & 0 & 0 & 1 \\ 0 & 1 & 0 & 0 & 0 \end{bmatrix}$$

1.2   Eulerian digraphs

Recall that a connected digraph is *Eulerian* if there is a closed trail that includes every arc just once; such a trail is called an *Eulerian trail*. For example, the following digraph is Eulerian; an Eulerian trail is *abcdefbgcegfa*.

Graphs 1, Section 3.4.

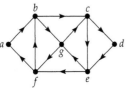

You met this digraph in *Graphs 1*. It is digraph (a) at the beginning of Section 3.4.

As for connected graphs, we can give a necessary and sufficient condition for a connected digraph to be Eulerian.

Theorem 1.3

A connected digraph is Eulerian if and only if, for each vertex, the out-degree equals the in-degree.

Graphs 1, Theorem 3.2.

Problem 1.5

(a) For the above digraph, write down the adjacency matrix **A**, and also the in-degree and out-degree for each vertex.

(b) Comment on your results.

Recall that if **A** is the adjacency matrix of a digraph, then the sum of the entries in any *row* of **A** is the *out-degree* of the corresponding vertex, and the sum of the entries in any *column* is the *in-degree* of the corresponding vertex. It follows that we can easily determine the out-degree and the in-degree of each vertex directly from the adjacency matrix, and thus determine whether the digraph may be Eulerian. To show that a digraph is Eulerian, we must also show that it is *connected*. We can show that a digraph is connected either by inspection of the adjacency matrix, or by showing that it is *strongly* connected, using Theorem 1.2.

Graphs 1, Section 4.1.

Problem 1.6

Consider the following adjacency matrix **A**.

$$
\begin{array}{c@{\quad}c}
 & \begin{matrix} a & b & c & d & e \end{matrix} \\
\begin{matrix} a \\ b \\ c \\ d \\ e \end{matrix} &
\begin{bmatrix}
0 & 1 & 0 & 0 & 0 \\
0 & 0 & 1 & 0 & 0 \\
1 & 0 & 0 & 0 & 1 \\
0 & 0 & 1 & 0 & 0 \\
0 & 0 & 0 & 1 & 0
\end{bmatrix}
\end{array}
$$

The matrix row and column headings are the vertex labels of the digraph.

Write down the out-degree and the in-degree of each vertex of the corresponding digraph D, and hence determine whether D is Eulerian. Check your answer by drawing the digraph D.

Once we have checked that an adjacency matrix represents an Eulerian digraph, we can find an Eulerian trail directly from the adjacency matrix. The method depends on the following result.

Theorem 1.4

An Eulerian digraph can be split into cycles, no two of which have an arc in common.

Graphs 1, Theorem 3.3.

To find an Eulerian trail in an Eulerian digraph, the first step is to find a cycle C_1 in the digraph. Either this is an Eulerian trail, or the removal of this cycle leaves a digraph in which the out-degree and in-degree are still equal for each vertex. We can therefore find another cycle C_2 in the resulting digraph. Continuing in this way, we eventually split the digraph into cycles. Finally, we join these cycles together to give the required Eulerian trail.

The digraph is Eulerian, so the out-degree and in-degree of each vertex are equal. In a cycle, the out-degree and in-degree of each vertex is 1.

We illustrate how to do this, working directly with the adjacency matrix, in the following worked problem.

Worked problem 1.1

Find an Eulerian trail in the digraph D with the adjacency matrix $\mathbf{A}$ shown in the margin.

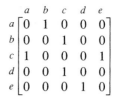

$$\begin{array}{c@{}c} & \begin{array}{ccccc} a & b & c & d & e \end{array} \\ \begin{array}{c} a \\ b \\ c \\ d \\ e \end{array} & \left[\begin{array}{ccccc} 0 & 1 & 0 & 0 & 0 \\ 0 & 0 & 1 & 0 & 0 \\ 1 & 0 & 0 & 0 & 1 \\ 0 & 0 & 1 & 0 & 0 \\ 0 & 0 & 0 & 1 & 0 \end{array}\right] \end{array}$$

Solution

We have shown in Problem 1.6 that the digraph D is Eulerian. We now look for a cycle in D by examining $\mathbf{A}$.

We first choose any non-zero entry in $\mathbf{A}$; let us choose the entry a_{12} (the entry in row 1 and column 2). We start the cycle with an arc from a to b, and reduce a_{12} by 1 (to 0).

An Eulerian trail contains each arc just *once*, so once we have used an arc in a cycle, we need to make sure that we do not use it again. We therefore reduce the corresponding entry in $\mathbf{A}$ by 1.

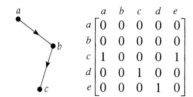

$$\begin{array}{c@{}c} & \begin{array}{ccccc} a & b & c & d & e \end{array} \\ \begin{array}{c} a \\ b \\ c \\ d \\ e \end{array} & \left[\begin{array}{ccccc} 0 & 0 & 0 & 0 & 0 \\ 0 & 0 & 1 & 0 & 0 \\ 1 & 0 & 0 & 0 & 1 \\ 0 & 0 & 1 & 0 & 0 \\ 0 & 0 & 0 & 1 & 0 \end{array}\right] \end{array}$$

We now want an arc from b, so we consider row 2 (the row with vertex label b) and choose any non-zero entry; the only possibility is the entry a_{23} in column 3 (the column with vertex label c). We continue the cycle with an arc from b to c, and reduce a_{23} by 1 (to 0).

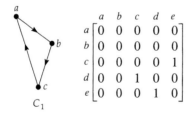

$$\begin{array}{c@{}c} & \begin{array}{ccccc} a & b & c & d & e \end{array} \\ \begin{array}{c} a \\ b \\ c \\ d \\ e \end{array} & \left[\begin{array}{ccccc} 0 & 0 & 0 & 0 & 0 \\ 0 & 0 & 0 & 0 & 0 \\ 1 & 0 & 0 & 0 & 1 \\ 0 & 0 & 1 & 0 & 0 \\ 0 & 0 & 0 & 1 & 0 \end{array}\right] \end{array}$$

We next want an arc from c, so we consider row 3 and choose any non-zero entry; let us choose the entry a_{31}. We continue the cycle with an arc from c to a, and reduce a_{31} by 1 (to 0). This completes the first cycle C_1: $abca$.

$$\begin{array}{c@{}c} & \begin{array}{ccccc} a & b & c & d & e \end{array} \\ \begin{array}{c} a \\ b \\ c \\ d \\ e \end{array} & \left[\begin{array}{ccccc} 0 & 0 & 0 & 0 & 0 \\ 0 & 0 & 0 & 0 & 0 \\ 0 & 0 & 0 & 0 & 1 \\ 0 & 0 & 1 & 0 & 0 \\ 0 & 0 & 0 & 1 & 0 \end{array}\right] \end{array}$$

C_1

We repeat the process, choosing a non-zero entry and building up another cycle, arc by arc. For example, starting with the non-zero entry in row 4, we obtain arcs from d to c, c to e, and e to d, thus completing another cycle C_2: $dced$.

C_2

Each entry in the matrix is now zero, indicating that there are no more arcs and hence no more cycles.

We finally obtain an Eulerian trail by joining these cycles together at c. We do this by replacing c in C_1 by C_2, after writing C_2 as $cedc$. This gives the Eulerian trail $abcedca$.

C_1: $abca$

C_2: $cedc$

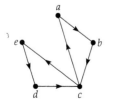

■

We now give a formal statement of the algorithm for finding Eulerian trails directly from the adjacency matrix.

Algorithm for finding an Eulerian trail in a digraph

To find an Eulerian trail in a digraph D with no loops, and adjacency matrix **A**, carry out the following steps.

START   Set cycle counter $p = 0$.

STEP 1   Increase p by 1.

Find a row k with a non-zero entry.

Set $n = k$ and put vertex v_k at the start of a cycle: $C_p = v_k \ldots$.

STEP 2   Choose m such that $a_{nm} > 0$.

Include vertex v_m as the next vertex in cycle C_p.

Reduce a_{nm} by 1.

Set $n = m$.

If $n \neq k$, return to the beginning of Step 2.

If $n = k$ and not all elements of **A** have been reduced to zero, store the cycle C_p and return to Step 1; otherwise go to Step 3.

STEP 3   If there is only one stored cycle, this is the required Eulerian trail. STOP.

Otherwise, in the set of stored cycles, find two cycles C_i and C_j with at least one vertex v in common. In C_i, replace the vertex v by C_j, after writing C_j in the form $C_j = v \ldots v$.

Delete C_j from the set of stored cycles.

Repeat this process until a single closed trail remains — this is the required Eulerian trail. STOP.

Note that when two cycles are combined the result is not a cycle.

Problem 1.7

Find an Eulerian trail in the digraph with the following adjacency matrix **A**. Start with the entry a_{12}.

An Eulerian trail in this digraph was found in Graphs 1, Problem 3.13(b).

$$
\begin{array}{c}
\\ a \\ b \\ c \\ d \\ e
\end{array}
\begin{array}{c}
\begin{array}{ccccc} a & b & c & d & e \end{array} \\
\begin{bmatrix}
0 & 1 & 1 & 0 & 0 \\
0 & 0 & 0 & 1 & 1 \\
0 & 1 & 0 & 1 & 0 \\
1 & 0 & 0 & 0 & 1 \\
1 & 0 & 1 & 0 & 0
\end{bmatrix}
\end{array}
$$

1.3   Hamiltonian digraphs

Recall that a connected digraph is Hamiltonian if there is a cycle which passes through every vertex; thus in a digraph with n vertices a Hamiltonian cycle has length n. Unfortunately, we have no general method of testing whether a given adjacency matrix is that of a Hamiltonian digraph.

Graphs 1, Section 3.4.

However, we can find Hamiltonian cycles in a digraph D with no loops directly from its adjacency matrix. We demonstrate this method by the following worked problem.

Worked problem 1.2

Find all the paths, cycles and Hamiltonian cycles in the digraph with the following adjacency matrix.

$$\begin{array}{c} & \begin{array}{cccc} a & b & c & d \end{array} \\ \begin{array}{c} a \\ b \\ c \\ d \end{array} & \left[\begin{array}{cccc} 0 & 1 & 0 & 1 \\ 0 & 0 & 1 & 1 \\ 1 & 0 & 0 & 0 \\ 0 & 0 & 1 & 0 \end{array}\right] \end{array}$$

We give the digraph so that you can appreciate the significance of the tables shown below.

Solution

The digraph has four vertices, so we wish to find all the cycles of length 4.

One systematic way of proceeding is to list all the paths which start from each vertex. Thus, working from the digraph or the adjacency matrix, we can record all paths of length 1 (arcs) in the digraph as follows.

	a	b	c	d
a	–	ab	–	ad
b	–	–	bc	bd
c	ca	–	–	–
d	–	–	dc	–

paths of length 1

The entry ab in row 1 and column 2 denotes a path from a to b.

Similarly, we can record all paths and cycles of length 2 as follows.

	a	b	c	d
a	–	–	abc adc	abd
b	bca	–	bdc	–
c	–	cab	–	cad
d	dca	–	–	–

paths of length 2

The entry abc in row 1 and column 3 denotes a path from a to b to c.

Note that the paths from a to c (abc and adc) both belong to the same cell of the matrix.

Next, we record all paths and cycles of length 3 as follows.

	a	b	c	d
a	abca adca	–	abdc	–
b	bdca	bcab	–	bcad
c	–	–	cabc cadc	cabd
d	–	dcab	–	dcad

paths of length 3

Finally, we record the Hamiltonian cycles — the cycles of length 4.

	a	b	c	d
a	abdca	–	–	–
b	–	bdcab	–	–
c	–	–	cabdc	–
d	–	–	–	dcabd

cycles of length 4

In fact, these cycles are all the same, so there is only one Hamiltonian cycle, $abdca$. ■

The algorithm for this problem generates matrices of the same form as the tables shown above. The entries are called **strings** and the matrices are combined by *latin multiplication* (denoted by #), which is similar to matrix multiplication with the strings combined as follows:

We have chosen a character on the computer keyboard that is not already being used as an operator — hence the unusual use of #.

- string multiplication *concatenates* the strings; for example,

$$v_1 v_2 v_4 \times v_3 v_5 = v_1 v_2 v_4 v_3 v_5$$

- string additions are written one above the other; for example,

$$v_1 v_2 v_4 + v_3 v_5 v_6 = \begin{matrix} v_1 v_2 v_4 \\ v_3 v_5 v_6 \end{matrix}$$

- a string which includes a vertex more than once is 0 unless such a vertex occurs *just* at the beginning and the end; for example,

$$v_1 v_2 v_1 v_3 = 0$$

$$v_1 v_2 v_3 v_1 \neq 0$$

- $0 \times$ (anything) = 0

- 0 + (something) = (something)

Problem 1.8

Find the matrix products $\mathbf{C}^2 = \mathbf{C} \, \# \, \mathbf{D}$, $\mathbf{C}^3 = \mathbf{C}^2 \, \# \, \mathbf{D}$ and $\mathbf{C}^4 = \mathbf{C}^3 \, \# \, \mathbf{D}$, using latin multiplication, where

$$\mathbf{C} = \begin{bmatrix} 0 & ab & 0 & ad \\ 0 & 0 & bc & bd \\ ca & 0 & 0 & 0 \\ 0 & 0 & dc & 0 \end{bmatrix} \quad \text{and} \quad \mathbf{D} = \begin{bmatrix} 0 & b & 0 & d \\ 0 & 0 & c & d \\ a & 0 & 0 & 0 \\ 0 & 0 & c & 0 \end{bmatrix}$$

Hint The element in row 1 and column 3 of $\mathbf{C} \, \# \, \mathbf{D}$ is obtained by adding the four products

$$0 \times 0 = 0, \quad ab \times c = abc, \quad 0 \times 0 = 0, \quad ad \times c = adc;$$

so this entry is $\begin{matrix} abc \\ adc \end{matrix}$.

We now give a formal statement of the algorithm for finding Hamiltonian cycles directly from the adjacency matrix.

Algorithm for finding Hamiltonian cycles in a digraph

To find all the Hamiltonian cycles in a digraph with n vertices and no loops, carry out the following steps.

STEP 1   Define an $n \times n$ matrix $\mathbf{C}$ as follows.

Put

$c_{ij} = v_i v_j$, if there is an arc from v_i to v_j,

$c_{ij} = 0$, otherwise.

There is an arc from v_i to v_j whenever the entry a_{ij} in the adjacency matrix $\mathbf{A}$ is non-zero.

Define an $n \times n$ matrix $\mathbf{D}$ to be the matrix obtained from $\mathbf{C}$ by deleting the first vertex in each non-zero entry of $\mathbf{C}$.

Set $k = 1$, where k is the power to which the matrix $\mathbf{C}$ is raised.

STEP 2   Form $\mathbf{C}^{k+1} = \mathbf{C}^k \, \# \, \mathbf{D}$, where # denotes latin multiplication.

$\mathbf{C}^1 = \mathbf{C}, \mathbf{C}^2 = \mathbf{C}^1 \, \# \, \mathbf{D}$.

STEP 3   If $k+1 \neq n$, increase k by 1 and return to Step 2.

If $k+1 = n$, STOP.

The entries in $\mathbf{C}^k$ give the paths of length k, for $k = 1, \ldots, n$.

The entries in $\mathbf{C}^n$ give the Hamiltonian cycles.

We now repeat the previous worked problem using the above algorithm.

Worked problem 1.3

Find all the Hamiltonian cycles in the digraph with the adjacency matrix **A** shown in the margin.

$$\mathbf{A} = \begin{array}{c} \\ a \\ b \\ c \\ d \end{array}\begin{array}{cccc} a & b & c & d \\ \begin{bmatrix} 0 & 1 & 0 & 1 \\ 0 & 0 & 1 & 1 \\ 1 & 0 & 0 & 0 \\ 0 & 0 & 1 & 0 \end{bmatrix} \end{array}$$

Solution

The digraph has four vertices, so a Hamiltonian cycle has length 4, and $n = 4$.

STEP 1   The matrix **C** is as follows.

$$\mathbf{C} = \begin{bmatrix} 0 & ab & 0 & ad \\ 0 & 0 & bc & bd \\ ca & 0 & 0 & 0 \\ 0 & 0 & dc & 0 \end{bmatrix}$$

The entries in **C** are the paths of length 1.

Deleting the first vertex of each non-zero entry of **C**, we obtain

$$\mathbf{D} = \begin{bmatrix} 0 & b & 0 & d \\ 0 & 0 & c & d \\ a & 0 & 0 & 0 \\ 0 & 0 & c & 0 \end{bmatrix}$$

Set $k = 1$ and write $\mathbf{C}^1 = \mathbf{C}$.

STEP 2   We form $\mathbf{C}^2 = \mathbf{C} \# \mathbf{D}$.

You found $\mathbf{C}^2$ in Problem 1.8.

$$\mathbf{C}^2 = \begin{bmatrix} 0 & 0 & \begin{matrix} abc \\ adc \end{matrix} & abd \\ bca & 0 & bdc & 0 \\ 0 & cab & 0 & cad \\ dca & 0 & 0 & 0 \end{bmatrix}$$

The entries in $\mathbf{C}^2$ are the paths of length 2.

STEP 3   Since $k + 1 = 2$ and $n = 4$, $k + 1 \neq n$, so set $k = 2$.

STEP 2   We form $\mathbf{C}^3 = \mathbf{C}^2 \# \mathbf{D}$.

You found $\mathbf{C}^3$ in Problem 1.8.

$$\mathbf{C}^3 = \begin{bmatrix} \begin{matrix} abca \\ adca \end{matrix} & 0 & abdc & 0 \\ bdca & bcab & 0 & bcad \\ 0 & 0 & \begin{matrix} cabc \\ cadc \end{matrix} & cabd \\ 0 & dcab & 0 & dcad \end{bmatrix}$$

The entries in $\mathbf{C}^3$ are the paths and cycles of length 3.

STEP 3   Since $k + 1 = 3$ and $n = 4$, $k + 1 \neq n$, so set $k = 3$.

STEP 2   We form $\mathbf{C}^4 = \mathbf{C}^3 \# \mathbf{D}$.

You found $\mathbf{C}^4$ in Problem 1.8.

$$\mathbf{C}^4 = \begin{bmatrix} abdca & 0 & 0 & 0 \\ 0 & bdcab & 0 & 0 \\ 0 & 0 & cabdc & 0 \\ 0 & 0 & 0 & dcabd \end{bmatrix}$$

The entries in $\mathbf{C}^4$ are the paths and cycles of length 4.

STEP 3   Since $k + 1 = 4 = n$, STOP.

The entries in $\mathbf{C}^4$ are all the same, so there is only one Hamiltonian cycle, $abdca$.   ∎

14

Problem 1.9

Find all the Hamiltonian cycles in the digraph with the adjacency matrix **A** shown in the margin.

$$\begin{array}{c} \\ a \\ b \\ c \\ d \end{array} \begin{array}{cccc} a & b & c & d \\ \begin{bmatrix} 0 & 1 & 0 & 1 \\ 1 & 0 & 0 & 1 \\ 1 & 1 & 0 & 0 \\ 0 & 0 & 1 & 0 \end{bmatrix} \end{array}$$

1.4 Computer activities

The computer activities for this section are described in the *Computer Activities Booklet*.

> After studying this section, you should be able to use the adjacency matrix of a given digraph to:
>
> - determine the number of walks from one given vertex of the digraph to another;
>
> - determine whether the digraph is strongly connected;
>
> - determine whether the digraph is Eulerian;
>
> - find an Eulerian trail in an Eulerian digraph with no loops, using the given algorithm;
>
> - find all the Hamiltonian cycles (if any) in a digraph with no loops, using the given algorithm.

2 Optimal path algorithms

2.1 Shortest and longest paths

In this section we consider problems which involve finding the longest or shortest paths in a network. There are two audio-tape sequences. In the first we describe the *shortest path algorithm* and in the second show how it can be modified to find the *longest path* in a network without cycles. This *longest path algorithm* forms the basis of the algorithm we shall use in Section 3 to find a 'critical path' in an 'activity network' for problems on scheduling.

> Now listen to bands 2 and 3 of Audio-tape 2. The associated frames are in *Audio-tape Notes 2*.

2.2 Computer activities

The computer activities for this section are described in the *Computer Activities Booklet*.

> After studying this section, you should be able to:
>
> - apply the shortest path algorithm to find the shortest path(s) between two vertices in a weighted digraph;
>
> - apply the longest path algorithm to find the longest path(s) between two vertices in a weighted digraph without cycles.

3 Critical path analysis

In Sections 3 and 4 we describe the use of network analysis in planning and scheduling the activities involved in large-scale projects such as those occurring in industry. The methods of solution to these problems are given as algorithms.

These network problems are, in general, considerably more complex than those we have studied earlier. A characteristic of many of the scheduling problems which we discuss is that there are no known efficient algorithms for finding optimum solutions.

Any project which can be broken down into separate activities interrelated in time can be represented by a network called an **activity network**. An example is shown in the following figure, which is an activity network for the construction of a small building such as a garage. Here the vertices represent separate activities involved in the project, and are numbered as well as having the activity label. The number next to each arc is the completion time of the activity represented by the vertex at the beginning of that arc. We use this building construction as an illustrative example throughout this section.

We explain the significance of the numbers on the vertices shortly.

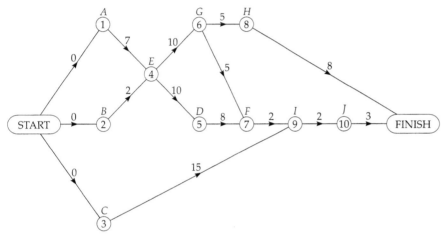

activity network for building construction

We shall show how the *minimum completion time* for the whole project can be determined by finding a *longest path*, called a *critical path*, through the corresponding activity network.

Many companies use network analysis as an aid to the planning and control of large-scale projects. The first forms of network analysis were devised and used in the USA in the late 1950s. Since that time, many different systems of network analysis have been developed which use the same basic techniques.

An essential part of these systems is the use of an activity network to represent a project. Once an activity network has been constructed, we can find a critical path, which tells us the minimum completion time for the project. We can then calculate the earliest and latest times by which each activity must begin if the project is not to be delayed.

Two types of activity network are in common use. Here we use the type in which each vertex represents an *activity* (as in the above example). Later in this section we describe the other type, in which each vertex represents an *event* (a stage in the process corresponding to the start or finish of one or more activities), and give a brief comparison of the two types.

Note that, throughout *this section*, we assume that *there is no restriction on the number of workers available*.

In Section 4 we investigate the problem of scheduling activities for a given number of workers.

3.1 Activity networks using vertices to represent activities

We begin by considering the project to construct a garage. The separate activities involved, and their estimated durations, are given in the following table.

activity	duration (in days)
A prepare foundations	7
B make and position doorframe	2
C lay drains, floor base and screed	15
D install services and fittings	8
E erect walls	10
F plaster ceiling	2
G erect roof	5
H install doors and windows, and paint outside	8
I fit gutters and pipes	2
J paint inside	3

Clearly, some of these activities cannot be started until other activities have been completed. For example, with the traditional methods of building, activity G (erect roof) cannot begin until activity E (erect walls) has been completed.

The following list of *precedence relations* shows which activities must precede which.

> D must follow E
>
> E must follow A and B
>
> F must follow D and G
>
> G must follow E
>
> H must follow G
>
> I must follow C and F
>
> J must follow I

In each of our examples, we simply *state* a list of precedence relations. We do not discuss the problem of actually obtaining a minimal list (that is, a list containing no redundant information) of precedence relations for a given project. Note, however, that redundancies in the precedence relations lead to redundant arcs in the activity network (see Problem 3.1).

We can represent this process of construction by the activity network given at the beginning of the section.

In this type of activity network, each activity is represented by a numbered vertex. An arc joining a vertex X to a vertex Y indicates that the activity represented by X must be completed before the activity represented by Y can be started. The number associated with an arc is the duration of the activity from which that arc is incident. For example, the arc joining A to E indicates that activity E must follow activity A, and the number 7 next to the arc is the duration (in days) of activity A. The activity network thus represents the precedence relations in diagrammatic form.

Notice that the activity network has a START vertex and a FINISH vertex — these do not represent any activities, but are included to complete the network. Since the START vertex does not represent an activity, the duration time associated with each arc leading from that vertex is zero.

An activity network can be used to find the minimum time necessary for the completion of the project it represents. Before showing how this is done, we present a systematic method for constructing an activity network from a table of precedence relations.

Algorithm for constructing an activity network

The following algorithm is a systematic procedure for numbering the activities and then drawing the activity network. One of the advantages of using this method rather than drawing the activity network by trial and error is that it produces a clear diagram in which the vertices are placed in a logical order.

The algorithm is in two parts:

Part A of the algorithm is a procedure developed by D. R. Fulkerson for numbering the activities and the corresponding vertices. The activities are numbered in such a way that each activity is assigned a number greater than the number assigned to any activity which must precede it.

Part B of the algorithm is a procedure for drawing the activity network.

Activity network construction algorithm

Part A: procedure for numbering the vertices

START   Represent each activity by a vertex.

For each vertex, create a **shadow vertex**, so that for each activity there are two corresponding vertices — the original vertex and the shadow vertex.

Construct a bipartite graph in which one set of vertices consists of the original vertices, and the other set consists of the shadow vertices.

original vertices	shadow vertices
$A \bullet$	$\circ A$
$B \bullet$	$\circ B$
$C \bullet$	$\circ C$
$\vdots$	$\vdots$
$N \bullet$	$\circ N$

If an activity Y must follow an activity X, draw an edge joining the original vertex representing Y to the shadow vertex representing X.

STEP 1   Number consecutively all the original vertices (chosen in any order) which have no edges incident with them. Record the numbering, together with the iteration number.

STEP 2   Delete all numbered vertices, their corresponding shadow vertices, and all edges incident with these vertices.

If not all the vertices have been numbered, return to Step 1.

If all the vertices have been numbered, go to Part B, Step 3.

Part B: procedure for drawing the activity network

STEP 3   Draw a START vertex, and the vertices numbered in the first iteration.

Draw an arc from the START vertex to each vertex which was numbered in the first iteration.

Assign a weight of zero to each arc.

STEP 4   Draw the vertices which were numbered in the next iteration.

To each such vertex Y, draw an arc from each previously numbered vertex X if there is an edge joining the original vertex Y to the shadow vertex X in the original bipartite graph constructed in Part A.

Assign a weight to each arc XY equal to the duration of the activity X.

Repeat until all vertices have been included in the activity network.

STEP 5   Draw a FINISH vertex.

From each terminal vertex Z (that is, each vertex whose out-degree is zero), draw an arc to the FINISH vertex.

Assign a weight to each such arc equal to the duration of the corresponding activity Z. STOP.

The activity network has now been constructed.

We illustrate the above procedure by using it to construct an activity network for the building construction example.

Worked problem 3.1

Construct an activity network for the building construction example, using the above algorithm. The activities and precedence relations are repeated below.

activity		duration (in days)	preceding activities
A	prepare foundations	7	
B	make and position doorframe	2	
C	lay drains, floor base and screed	15	
D	install services and fittings	8	E
E	erect walls	10	A, B
F	plaster ceiling	2	D, G
G	erect roof	5	E
H	install doors and windows, and paint outside	8	G
I	fit gutters and pipes	2	C, F
J	paint inside	3	I

Solution

Part A: procedure for numbering the vertices

START We draw a bipartite graph with a vertex in each set corresponding to each activity, the original vertex in one set and a corresponding shadow vertex in the other set.

We draw an edge joining an original vertex to one of the shadow vertices if the activity corresponding to the original vertex must follow the activity represented by the shadow vertex.

We thus obtain the following bipartite graph representing the precedence relations.

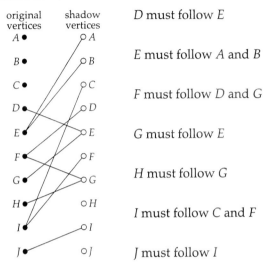

original vertices   shadow vertices

D must follow E

E must follow A and B

F must follow D and G

G must follow E

In the bipartite graph an edge joins the original vertex representing an activity to the shadow vertex representing an activity which must precede it.

H must follow G

I must follow C and F

J must follow I

First iteration

STEP 1 The original vertices which have no edges incident with them are A, B and C. Thus we assign the number 1 to vertex A, 2 to vertex B, and 3 to vertex C, as shown on the left below.

STEP 2 We delete the numbered vertices, the corresponding shadow vertices and all the edges incident with them. We are left with the graph shown on the right below.

RECORD:

iteration 1
A 1
B 2
C 3

original vertices   shadow vertices

STEP 1   STEP 2

Second iteration

STEP 1 The only original vertex which has no edge incident with it is vertex E, so we number this vertex 4 as shown on the left below.

STEP 2 We delete the vertex E, its shadow vertex and the edges incident with it. We are left with the graph shown on the right below.

RECORD:

iteration 2
E 4

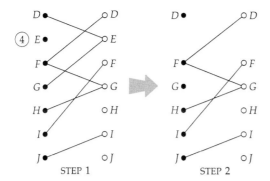

Third iteration

STEP 1   We number vertices D and G as shown on the left below.

STEP 2   We delete vertices D and G, their shadow vertices and the edges incident with them. We are left with the graph shown on the right below.

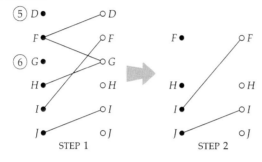

Fourth iteration

STEP 1   We number the vertices F and H as shown on the left below.

STEP 2   We delete vertices F and H, their shadow vertices and the edge incident with F. We are left with the graph shown on the right below.

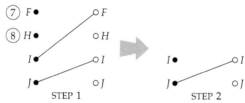

Fifth iteration

STEP 1   We number vertex I.

STEP 2   We delete vertex I, its shadow vertex and the remaining edge. We are left with only vertex J.

Sixth iteration

STEP 1   We number the remaining vertex J.

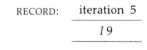

STEP 2   This completes Part A of the algorithm, as all the vertices have been numbered. We now proceed to Part B.

Part B: procedure for drawing the activity network

Using the information recorded when carrying out Part A, we construct the following activity network which we gave at the beginning of this section.

iteration	1	2	3	4	5	6
vertices	$A\,1$	$E\,4$	$D\,5$	$F\,7$	$I\,9$	$J\,10$
numbered	$B\,2$		$G\,6$	$H\,8$		
	$C\,3$					

The details of the construction of this network are given below.

STEP 3   We draw the START vertex, and the vertices numbered in the first iteration: A, B and C. We then draw arcs from the START vertex to A, B and C, assigning a zero weight to each.

We place the vertices drawn in each iteration in vertical columns.

STEP 4   In the second iteration we numbered vertex E, so we add vertex E to the activity network.

From the original bipartite graph showing the precedence relations, we see that A and B must precede E, so we draw arcs:

from A to E, with weight 7 (the duration of A);
from B to E, with weight 2 (the duration of B).

STEP 4   In the third iteration we numbered vertices D and G, so we add vertices D and G to the activity network.

Activity E must precede D and G, so we draw arcs:

from E to D, with weight 10 (the duration of E);
from E to G, with weight 10 (the duration of E).

We have placed vertex G above vertex D to avoid later arcs of the network crossing. (Hindsight!)

STEP 4   In the fourth iteration we numbered vertices F and H, so we add vertices F and H to the activity network.

Activities D and G must precede F, and activity G must precede H, so we draw arcs:

from D to F, with weight 8 (the duration of D);
from G to F, with weight 5 (the duration of G);
from G to H, with weight 5 (the duration of G).

STEP 4   In the fifth iteration we numbered vertex I, so we add vertex I to the activity network.

Activities C and F must precede I, so we draw arcs:

from C to I, with weight 15 (the duration of C);
from F to I, with weight 2 (the duration of F).

STEP 4   In the sixth iteration, we numbered vertex J, so we add vertex J to the activity network.

Activity *I* must precede *J*, so we draw an arc:

from *I* to *J*, with weight 2 (the duration of *I*).

All the activities have now been represented by vertices in the activity network.

STEP 5   We draw a FINISH vertex.

From **the** terminal vertices *H* and *J*, we draw arcs:

from *H* to FINISH, with weight 8 (the duration of *H*);
from *J* to FINISH, with weight 3 (the duration of *J*).

The activity network is now complete and is the one given at the beginning of this section. ■

Note that, as well as ordering the activities, the procedure in Part A enables us to detect any inconsistencies in the precedence relations. For example, suppose that we are given the following precedence relations.

B must follow A

A must follow C

C must fol B

To start the algorithm, we construct the above graph, but we cannot proceed with Step 1, because there are no isolated vertices. The activities form a cycle, so it is impossible to schedule them, since none of the activities can be started. If a cycle arises from a list of precedence relations, then such relations are not compatible with a feasible schedule. The presence of a cycle is revealed by the numbering procedure, since no numbers can be assigned to any of the vertices representing activities of the cycle.

Problem 3.1

The process of assembling a bicycle is divided into the following activities. The precedence relations are also shown in the table.

activity		duration (in minutes)	preceding activities
A	prepare frame, including front fork	7	
B	mount and align front wheel	7	
C	mount and align back wheel	7	D, E
D	attach dérailleur to frame	2	
E	install gear cluster	3	D
F	attach chain wheel to crank	2	D
G	attach crank and chain wheel to frame	2	F
H	mount right pedal and toe-clip	8	E, F, G
I	mount left pedal and toe-clip	8	E, F, G
J	make final attachments; fix and adjust handlebars, saddle and brakes	18	A, B, C, D, E

Use the algorithm to construct an activity network for this process.

Problem 3.2

The activity network you constructed in Problem 3.1 contains some redundant arcs. Which are they and which are the redundant precedence relations?

3.2 Activity networks using vertices to represent events

An alternative type of activity network uses arcs to represent activities and vertices to represent *events*. An **event** is a stage in the process corresponding to the start or finish of one or more activities. For example, if activities B and C must follow activity A, this can be represented as follows.

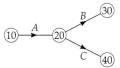

Vertices 10 and 20 represent the start and finish of activity A. The event 20 is also the start event for activities B and C. Activities are commonly referred to by quoting their start and finish event numbers; so, for example, activity C is referred to as activity 2040.

In the numbering procedure no vertex is numbered until the vertices at the tail of any arc pointing towards it have been numbered.

With this type of activity network, it is sometimes necessary to introduce **dummy activities**. For example, if activity C must follow activity A, and activity D must follow activities A and B, we would draw the activity network as follows.

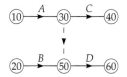

The dummy activity 3050, represented by the dashed line, is introduced to show that activity D cannot start until activity A has been completed. Dummy activities have no time duration. Note that this activity network is not the same as the following network, which represents the case when both C and D must follow both activities A and B.

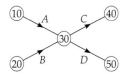

Dummy activities are also used when two activities have the same start and end events. This is done so that each activity can be referred to by a different number. An example is given below.

As an illustration, we give below an activity network with vertices representing events for the building construction example.

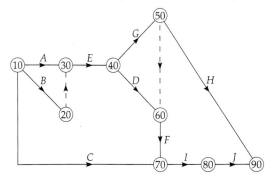

You may be wondering why the vertices of the activity network are numbered with such large numbers. The reason is that during the planning stage, or later, it may be necessary to include additional activities. The style of numbering adopted allows additional vertices to be conveniently numbered in the correct sequence.

24

3.3 Comparison of the two types of activity network

The first methods of network analysis to be developed used the type of activity network in which vertices represent events. Two methods of this type were developed at about the same time in the late 1950s and were the first to be used in the planning of large-scale industrial projects. These were PERT (Program Evaluation and Review Technique) and CPM (Critical Path Method). PERT was used by the US Navy to plan the Polaris missile project, where the main objective was to complete the project in the shortest possible time. This was a complex project involving activities whose times could not be accurately predicted. CPM was developed by the Du Pont de Nemours Company; here the primary concern was to minimize the total cost of a project. The most widely accepted distinction between PERT and CPM concerns the performance times for the activities. CPM is used for cases where these times can be predicted reasonably accurately. The important distinctive feature of PERT is that the technique permits probabilistic estimates of activity times, and so can accommodate research and developmental projects in which times for activities cannot be predicted with confidence. This means that it can also be used for projects which may suffer disruption through strike action or late delivery of materials.

The type of activity network in which vertices represent activities was developed by Bernard Roy of Metra International, a management consultancy firm. This type of activity network is easier to understand and easier to construct than the other type. In particular, it does not require the use of dummy activities. A disadvantage for some applications is that the events are not included in the network, which makes it more difficult to plan a number of concurrent projects.

In this unit we have chosen to introduce both types of activity network, but to concentrate on the type of activity network in which vertices represent activities, because its construction is more straightforward than for the other type. The analysis of both types of activity network have the same essential features and involve finding a 'critical path' in the network. Our aim is to explain the basic principles and techniques on which practical methods of network analysis such as PERT and CPM are based. However, both PERT and CPM involve complexities which cannot be included here.

The algorithms we give are in a form suitable for the type of activity network in which vertices represent activities. However, the same algorithms can be adapted, with only minor modifications, for the other type of activity network.

3.4 Critical paths

When planning a project, we usually need to know the minimum time needed to complete the project. We can calculate this *minimum completion time* from the activity network for the project. To do this, we find a longest path, called a **critical path**, from the START vertex to the FINISH vertex. By a **longest path** we mean a path for which the sum of the times associated with the arcs of the path (that is, the length of the path) has the largest possible value. The **minimum completion time** is equal to the **length of a critical path**.

A delay in completing any activity on a critical path delays the completion of the project by the same amount. *Note that an activity network may contain more than one critical path.*

A critical path can be found by inspection in a small activity network, but for larger examples we need a systematic method. Such a method is given below in the form of an algorithm.

Problem 3.3

What is the effect on the completion time of a project of a delay in the completion of an activity which is not on any critical path?

In the solution to the above problem we saw that an activity not on a critical path may be delayed by a certain amount without delaying the whole project. The maximum time by which an activity may be delayed without delaying the project is called the **float** of that activity.

If a project is to be completed in the shortest possible time, then particular attention must be paid to the activities on any critical path. For other activities, there is some leeway in their starting time or duration — the amount of leeway for such an activity is its float.

In Section 2 we discussed the problem of finding a longest path in a network. This problem is closely related to the problem of finding a critical path in an activity network, and we could use the longest path algorithm given in Section 2 to find a critical path in an activity network. However, because of the special structure of an *activity* network — namely, the way the vertices are numbered — we can improve on this method. The algorithm we now give for finding a critical path is more efficient than the longest path algorithm given in Section 2.

Algorithm for constructing critical paths

The algorithm for finding a critical path in an activity network is similar to the longest path algorithm, except that we make use of the numbering of the vertices in the activity network. We saw earlier that this numbering is possible only because an activity network contains no cycles.

The algorithm is in two parts:

Part A is a forward scan, in which vertices are labelled consecutively.

Part B is a backward scan, in which critical paths are identified.

We give a formal statement of the algorithm, and then illustrate its use with an example. We adopt the following notation.

Conventions

We assume that the network involves n activities. We regard the START vertex as the 0th vertex and the FINISH vertex as the $(n + 1)$th vertex.

The duration of activity i represented by the arc ij is denoted by $c_{i,j}$.

The algorithm assigns labels p_j and e_j to each vertex j for $j = 0, 1, ..., n + 1$. When the algorithm has been completed:

e_j is the length of the longest path from the START vertex to vertex j;

p_j is the number of the preceding vertex on this longest path.

We shall see later that e_j is the 'earliest starting time' of the activity represented by vertex j; that is, the earliest time at which the activity can be started.

Critical path construction algorithm

In general, there may be more than one critical path. However, in each of our worked problems there is only one.

Part A: labelling procedure

STEP 1   Assign to the START vertex (vertex 0) the labels $p_0 = 0$ and $e_0 = 0$.

STEP 2   Carry out the following procedure for each vertex j, starting with $j = 1$ and continuing with $j = 2$, $j = 3$, and so on, until all the vertices (including the FINISH vertex, corresponding to $j = n + 1$) have been labelled.

For the current vertex j, calculate, for each arc ij incident to vertex j, the sum $e_i + c_{i,j}$.

Choose the maximum value of these sums for all such arcs ij, and set e_j equal to this value.

Set p_j equal to the value of i for which this sum is largest; in the case of a tie, choose any of the appropriate values.

Part B: tracing back procedure

STEP 3   Start with the FINISH vertex $n + 1$, and mark the arc joining this vertex to the preceding vertex p_{n+1}.

STEP 4   Consider the vertex j from which the last marked arc is incident. Mark the arc joining this vertex to the preceding vertex p_j.

Repeat until the START vertex is reached. STOP.

The marked arcs form a critical path.

The sum of the weights on the arcs of the critical path is the minimum completion time, and is given by the value of e_{n+1}.

We illustrate the above procedure by an example.

Worked problem 3.2

Find a critical path in the following activity network for the building construction example, using the critical path construction algorithm.

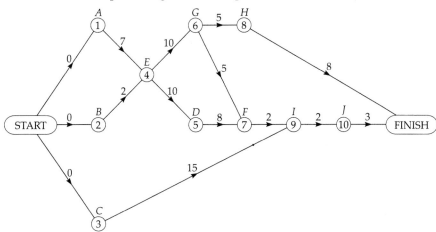

activity network for building construction

Solution

Part A: labelling procedure

STEP 1

Vertex 0   We label the START vertex with $p_0 = 0$ and $e_0 = 0$.

STEP 2   We consider each vertex in turn.

Vertex 1   There is only one arc incident to this vertex, so

$$e_1 = e_0 + c_{0,1} = 0 + 0 = 0.$$

We set p_1 equal to the number of the vertex from which the corresponding arc is incident, so

$$p_1 = 0.$$

Vertex 2   The situation is the same for these vertices as for vertex 1.

Vertex 3   The current labels are shown in the following diagram.

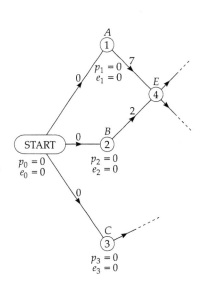

27

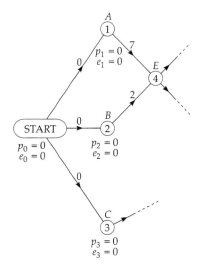

Vertex 4 There are two arcs incident to this vertex:

for the arc joining vertex 1 to vertex 4,

$$e_1 + c_{1,4} = 0 + 7 = 7;$$

for the arc joining vertex 2 to vertex 4,

$$e_2 + c_{2,4} = 0 + 2 = 2.$$

The larger of these sums is the first, so

$$e_4 = 7;$$
$$p_4 = 1.$$

Vertex 5 There is only one arc incident to vertex 5, from vertex 4, so

$$e_5 = e_4 + c_{4,5} = 7 + 10 = 17;$$
$$p_5 = 4.$$

Vertex 6 There is only one arc incident to vertex 6, from vertex 4, so

$$e_6 = e_4 + c_{4,6} = 7 + 10 = 17;$$
$$p_6 = 4.$$

The labelling of vertices 4, 5 and 6 is shown on the following diagram.

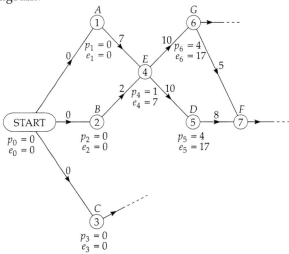

Vertex 7 There are two arcs incident to this vertex:

for the arc joining vertex 5 to vertex 7,

$$e_5 + c_{5,7} = 17 + 8 = 25;$$

for the arc joining vertex 6 to vertex 7,

$$e_6 + c_{6,7} = 17 + 5 = 22.$$

The larger of these sums is the first, so

$$e_7 = 25;$$
$$p_7 = 5.$$

Continuing in this way, but recording our values in a table, we assign labels to all the vertices. The resulting labels are shown in the diagram below the table.

j	i	e_i	$c_{i,j}$	$e_i + c_{i,j}$	e_j	p_j
0	–	–	–	–	0	0
1	0	0	0	0	0	0
2	0	0	0	0	0	0
3	0	0	0	0	0	0
4	1	0	7	7	7	1
4	2	0	2	2		
5	4	7	10	17	17	4
6	4	7	10	17	17	4
7	5	17	8	25	25	5
7	6	17	5	22		
8	6	17	5	22	22	6
9	3	0	15	15		
9	7	25	2	27	27	7
10	9	27	2	29	29	9
11	8	22	8	30		
11	10	29	3	32	32	10

Here j is the number of the vertex being labelled, and i is the number of any vertex from which there is an arc to vertex j.

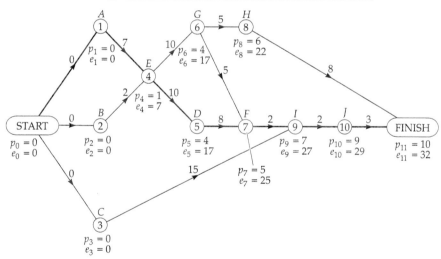

activity network for building construction

The critical path found in Part B below is marked on this diagram. We use thick lines to show a critical path in an activity network.

Part B: tracing back procedure

STEP 3   The FINISH vertex is vertex 11.

Since $p_{11} = 10$, we mark the arc from vertex 10 to the FINISH vertex.

STEP 4   Since $p_{10} = 9$, we mark the arc from vertex 9 to vertex 10.

STEP 4   Since $p_9 = 7$, we mark the arc from vertex 7 to vertex 9.

STEP 4   Since $p_7 = 5$, we mark the arc from vertex 5 to vertex 7.

STEP 4   Since $p_5 = 4$, we mark the arc from vertex 4 to vertex 5.

STEP 4   Since $p_4 = 1$, we mark the arc from vertex 1 to vertex 4.

STEP 4   Since $p_1 = 0$, we mark the arc from the START vertex to vertex 1.

The path obtained in Part B above may also be obtained by tracing back on the table from Part A as shown below.

In this example there is only one critical path. If there were more than one, this would be apparent from the p_j column (see Exercise 3.7).

j	i	e_i	$c_{i,j}$	$e_i + c_{i,j}$	e_j	p_j	activity numbered j
0	–	–	–	–	0	0	START
1 → 0	0	0	0	0	0	0	A
2	0	0	0	0	0	0	B
3	0	0	0	0	0	0	C
4 → 1	0	7	7	7	1	E
4	2	0	2	2			
5 → 4	7	10	17	17	4	D
6	4	7	10	17	17	4	G
7 → 5	17	8	25	25	5	F
7	6	17	5	22			
8	6	17	5	22	22	6	H
9	3	0	15	15			
9 → 7	25	2	27	27	7	I
10 → 9	27	2	29	29	9	J
11	8	22	8	30			
11 → 10	29	3	32	32	10	FINISH

The critical path is via vertices A, E, D, F, I and J. The length of the critical path is $0 + 7 + 10 + 8 + 2 + 2 + 3 = 32$, the value of e_{11}; thus the minimum completion time is 32 days. ∎

Problem 3.4

The activity network for the process of assembling a bicycle is reproduced below.

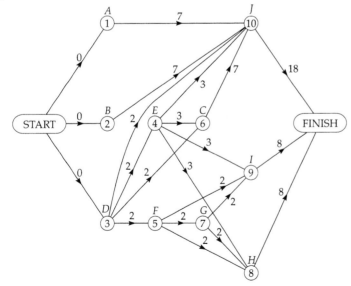

activity network for bicycle assembly

Use the critical path construction algorithm to find a critical path in the activity network, and calculate the minimum completion time of the project.

3.5 Earliest and latest starting times

The critical path construction algorithm assigns a label e_i to each vertex i. The value of e_i is the length of the longest path from the START vertex to the vertex i. In other words, e_i is the **earliest starting time** of activity i, since activity i cannot be started until all preceding activities have been completed. We can also calculate for each activity i the **latest starting time** l_i, which is the latest time at which activity i can be started without delaying the whole project.

Recall that the *float* of activity i is the maximum amount of time by which the activity can be delayed without delaying the project. Thus the float is the difference between these two times:

float of activity $i = l_i - e_i$.

For an activity i on the critical path, $e_i = l_i$. The float of an activity on the critical path is therefore zero.

Problem 3.5

In the following activity network, the critical path is indicated by thick lines, and the duration times are in days.

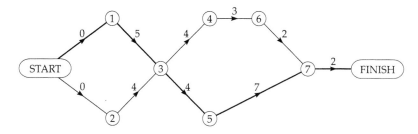

(a) What is the minimum completion time of the project?

(b) Calculate the earliest starting times for activities 4 and 6.

(c) Calculate the latest starting times for activities 6 and 4.

(d) Calculate the floats for activities 4 and 6.

(e) Can *both* activity 4 and activity 6 be delayed by their floats without delaying the completion of the project?

In the above problem, we calculated the latest starting times and the floats for two activities in a simple activity network. The following algorithm is a systematic method of calculating latest starting times for all the vertices. As in the solution to the above problem, we begin at the FINISH vertex and work back, vertex by vertex, until all the vertices have been considered.

Algorithm for calculating latest starting times

This algorithm is applied to an activity network (with n activities) for which we have calculated the minimum completion time. It is used to calculate the value of the latest starting time l_i for each vertex i, for $i = n + 1, n, ..., 1, 0$.

STEP 1   For vertex $n + 1$ (the FINISH vertex), set l_{n+1} equal to the minimum completion time.

STEP 2   Carry out the following procedure for each vertex i, starting with $i = n$ and continuing with $i = n - 1$, $i = n - 2$, and so on, until all the vertices including vertex 0 (the START vertex) have been considered.

For the current vertex i, calculate, for each arc ij incident from vertex i, the difference $l_j - c_{i,j}$, where $c_{i,j}$ is the duration of activity i.

Choose the minimum value of these differences for all such arcs ij, and set l_i equal to this value.

When the START vertex has been considered, STOP.

Note that l_0 must be zero — if we do not obtain this value, then we know that we have made a mistake somewhere.

We illustrate the above procedure by applying it to the activity network and critical path for the building construction example.

Worked problem 3.3

Use the algorithm to find the latest starting times for the building construction example. Hence find the float of each activity. The activity network and critical path are shown below.

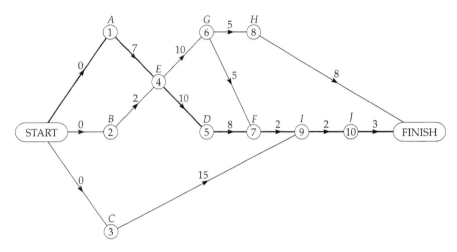

Solution

The minimum completion time is equal to the length of a critical path, so in this case it is 32 days.

We now apply the algorithm.

STEP 1   For vertex 11 (the FINISH vertex), we set l_{11} equal to the minimum completion time:

$$l_{11} = 32 \text{ days.}$$

STEP 2   We consider each vertex in turn.

Vertex 10   There is only one arc incident from this vertex, so

$$l_{10} = l_{11} - c_{10,11} = 32 - 3 = 29.$$

Similarly,

Vertex 9 $l_9 = l_{10} - c_{9,10} = 29 - 2 = 27;$

Vertex 8 $l_8 = l_{11} - c_{8,11} = 32 - 8 = 24;$

Vertex 7 $l_7 = l_9 - c_{7,9} = 27 - 2 = 25.$

Vertex 6   There are two arcs incident from this vertex. For the arc joining vertex 6 to vertex 8, the difference is

$$l_8 - c_{6,8} = 24 - 5 = 19,$$

and for the arc joining vertex 6 to vertex 7, the difference is

$$l_7 - c_{6,7} = 25 - 5 = 20.$$

The smaller of these differences is the first, so

$$l_6 = 19.$$

Vertex 5 Only one arc is incident from this vertex, so

$$l_5 = l_7 - c_{5,7} = 25 - 8 = 17.$$

Vertex 4 Two arcs are incident from this vertex. For the arc joining vertex 4 to vertex 6, the difference is

$$l_6 - l_{4,6} = 19 - 10 = 9,$$

and for the arc joining vertex 4 to vertex 5, the difference is

$$l_5 - l_{4,5} = 17 - 10 = 7.$$

The smaller of these difference is the second, so

$$l_4 = 7.$$

Vertex 3 Only one arc is incident from this vertex, so

$$l_3 = l_9 - c_{3,9} = 27 - 15 = 12.$$

Vertex 2 Only one arc is incident from this vertex, so

$$l_2 = l_4 - c_{2,4} = 7 - 2 = 5.$$

Vertex 1 Only one arc is incident from this vertex, so

$$l_1 = l_4 - c_{1,4} = 7 - 7 = 0.$$

Vertex 0 This is the START vertex. Three arcs are incident from this vertex. For the arc joining vertex 0 to vertex 3, the difference is

$$l_3 - c_{0,3} = 12 - 0 = 12,$$

for the arc joining vertex 0 to vertex 2, the difference is

$$l_2 - c_{0,2} = 5 - 0 = 5,$$

and for the arc joining vertex 0 to vertex 1, the difference is

$$l_1 - c_{0,1} = 0 - 0 = 0.$$

The smallest of these differences is the last, so

$$l_0 = 0,$$

as expected.

Alternatively, Step 2 of the algorithm can be set out in a table as shown below.

i	j	l_j	$c_{i,j}$	$l_j - c_{i,j}$	l_i
11	–	–	–	–	32
10	11	32	3	29	29
9	10	29	2	27	27
8	11	32	8	24	24
7	9	27	2	25	25
6	8	24	5	19	19
6	7	25	5	20	
5	7	25	8	17	17
4	6	19	10	9	
4	5	17	10	7	7
3	9	27	15	12	12
2	4	7	2	5	5
1	4	7	7	0	0
0	3	12	0	12	
0	2	5	0	5	
0	1	0	0	0	0

Notice that $l_0 = 0$.

The following table shows the earliest and latest starting times and the float of each activity in the building project.

activity numbered i	vertex number i	earliest starting time e_i	latest starting time l_i	float $l_i - e_i$
START	0	0	0	0
A	1	0	0	0
B	2	0	5	5
C	3	0	12	12
E	4	7	7	0
D	5	17	17	0
G	6	17	19	2
F	7	25	25	0
H	8	22	24	2
I	9	27	27	0
J	10	29	29	0
FINISH	11	32	32	0

Notice that, as stated above, any activity which is on a critical path has a float of zero — this must be so, since any delay in the completion of an activity on a critical path must delay the project. ∎

Problem 3.6

The activity network for the process of assembling a bicycle is reproduced below. The critical path is indicated by thick lines; the minimum completion time is 30 minutes.

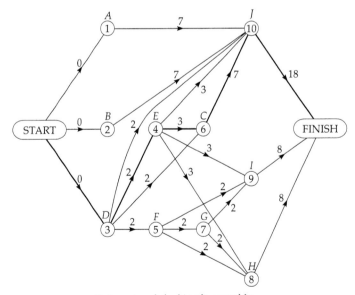

activity network for bicycle assembly

(a) Apply the algorithm for finding the latest starting times.

(b) Calculate the float for each activity.

Problem 3.7

A project consists of ten activities A–J. The duration of each activity and the activities that must precede each of them are as follows.

activity	duration (in days)	preceding activities
A	10	
B	4	
C	8	B
D	6	C
E	8	I
F	5	
G	10	A, D
H	2	G
I	4	
J	10	D, F, I

Using the algorithms:

(a) construct an activity network for this project;

(b) find a critical path and the minimum completion time;

(c) find the latest starting time and the float for each activity.

Before leaving the subject of activity networks, we mention an important difficulty which often arises in practice — namely that the estimated durations of the activities may not be accurate, or may vary during the planning and production stages. If estimates change, then the activity network must be updated and, if necessary, the calculations of earliest and latest starting times repeated. In particular, this may result in a different set of activities forming the critical path. The advantage of PERT is that at the planning stage three estimates of the time required may be specified for each activity — the *optimistic time*, the *most likely time*, and the *pessimistic time*. Moreover, software packages are available which will handle PERT calculations, thus facilitating the updating of the network, and the monitoring and control of the project once it is underway.

3.6 Computer activities

The computer activities for this section are described in the *Computer Activity Booklet*.

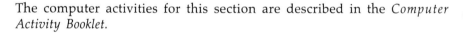

After studying this section, you should be able to:

(a) explain the terms *precedence relations, activity network, critical path, minimum completion time, earliest starting time, latest starting time* and *float*;

(b) distinguish between the two types of activity network in common use;

(c) apply the algorithm to construct an activity network from a table of precedence relations;

(d) find a critical path in an activity network by using the critical path construction algorithm, and calculate the minimum completion time;

(e) apply the algorithm to find the latest starting times from an activity network with a critical path, and calculate the float of each activity.

4   Scheduling

In the previous section we saw that the minimum completion time for a project is given by the length of a critical path in the corresponding activity network. This is the shortest time in which the project can be completed if there is no restriction on the number of workers available. However, if there is a limit on the number of workers available, it may not be possible to achieve this minimum completion time. If the product of this minimum completion time and the number of workers is less than the sum of the durations of all the activities, then it is obviously impossible to finish in the minimum completion time. Even if the product is not less than the sum of the durations, the precedence relations may be such that some workers will have idle periods, so that it is again impossible to finish in the minimum completion time.

In this section we investigate the problem of scheduling the activities of a project *for a given number of workers* in the shortest possible time.

4.1   Scheduling a project for a given number of workers

We suppose that an ideal schedule satisfies the following conditions, which we call the **factory rules**.

1   No worker may be idle if there is some activity which can be done.

2   Once a worker starts an activity, that activity must be continued by the same worker until it is completed.

3   The project must be completed as soon as possible with the manpower available.

These rules imply that the workers should have a minimum amount of idle time, and that activities on a critical path should be started as soon as possible.

Suppose, for example, that we wish to schedule the bicycle assembly project of the previous section for two workers according to the factory rules.

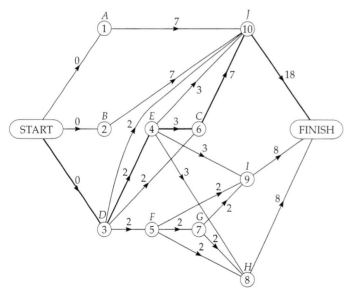

This activity network was constructed in Problem 3.1 and the critical path was determined in Problem 3.4.

activity network for bicycle assembly

As a first attempt at a schedule, let us assign all the activities on the critical path to worker 1, and all the remaining activities to worker 2. In doing this, we assign the activities in the order of the numbering scheme, taking into account the precedence relations involving activities done by both workers. In Problem 3.4 we showed that the activities on the critical path take a total of 30 minutes. Since the sum of the durations for all the activities is 64 minutes, the activities assigned to worker 2 take a total of 34 minutes to complete. So, if the activities are scheduled in this way, the shortest possible time for the completion of the project is 34 minutes. The actual time may be greater because of the precedence relations, which mean that some activities cannot be started until others have been completed.

The resulting schedule is the following.

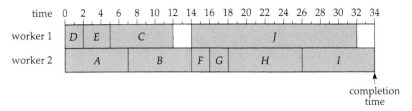

Note that worker 1 is idle for 2 minutes before starting activity J, because activity J cannot be started until activity B has been completed.

As it happens, this schedule does take 34 minutes — the minimum possible time which we calculated for this way of assigning activities. We notice that worker 1 is idle for two time intervals each of 2 minutes.

This schedule violates factory rule 1, since worker 1 could begin activity F as soon as he or she finishes activity C. It may also violate factory rule 3, since the absolute minimum completion time with two workers is 64/2 = 32 minutes.

We can improve on the above schedule by assigning activity F to worker 1 as soon as he or she completes activity C. We thus obtain the following schedule.

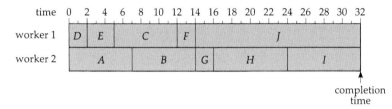

This schedule has a completion time of 32 minutes — it is an optimum schedule in the sense that it has the shortest possible completion time for any schedule for two workers. This schedule also satisfies all the factory rules.

We arrived at this optimum solution by a trial-and-error method. Is it possible to devise a systematic method which will produce an optimum schedule for any activity network with a given number of workers? The answer to this question appears to be 'no' — there is no known efficient algorithm for doing this. You may argue that, in principle, we can use the *exhaustion method*: list all possible schedules and choose one with a minimum completion time. However, the number of possible schedules grows so rapidly with the number of activities that there is no possibility of examining a small fraction of them, even using a computer, when the number of activities is large.

This is an example of the combinatorial explosion.

Since there is no practical algorithm for this type of scheduling problem, we use instead a *heuristic* method — that is, one depending on assumptions based on past experience. This method does not necessarily give an optimum solution, but usually gives a reasonable one. The following heuristic algorithm, called the *critical path scheduling algorithm*, has often been used in industry. It produces a schedule which satisfies the first two factory rules, but not necessarily the third rule.

Algorithm for scheduling activities

The algorithm assigns activities to a number of processors, which may be people or machines. It is assumed that the activity network has been constructed and the latest starting times calculated.

37

The algorithm makes use of a hypothetical clock to keep track of time. We call this the *project clock*. At the end of each iteration, we advance the project clock so that it records the time for which the project has been running.

Critical path scheduling algorithm

START Set the project clock to 0.

STEP 1 If at least one processor is free, assign to any free processor the most critical unassigned activity which can be started.

Repeat until no processor is free or until no unassigned activity can be started.

The most critical activity is one with the smallest latest starting time.

STEP 2 Advance the project clock until a time is reached when at least one activity has been completed, so that at least one processor is free.

If not all the activities have been assigned, return to Step 1.

If all the activities have been assigned, advance the project clock until all the activities have been completed. STOP: the project clock gives the minimum completion time.

We illustrate the above procedure by an example.

Worked problem 4.1

Apply the critical path scheduling algorithm to the bicycle assembly project for two workers. The activity network for this project, and a list of the latest starting times and durations (in minutes) are as follows.

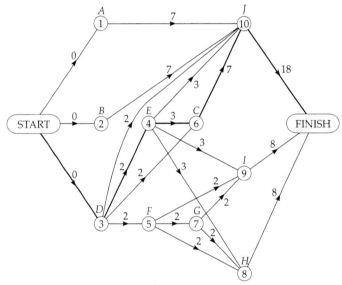

activity network for bicycle assembly

vertex number i	1	2	3	4	5	6	7	8	9	10
activity	A	B	D	E	F	C	G	H	I	J
duration	7	7	2	3	2	7	2	8	8	18
l_i	5	5	0	2	18	5	20	22	22	12

Solution

The steps involved in applying the algorithm are given below.

START Set the project clock to 0.

STEP 1 The activities which can be started are A, B and D. The most critical of these is activity D, since it has the smallest latest starting time. We therefore assign activity D to worker 1.

Activities *A* and *B* can be started, and both have the same latest starting time, so either can be chosen. We assign activity *A* to worker 2.

STEP 2 Advance the project clock to 2 minutes.

Activity *D* is completed, so worker 1 is free.

Activities *E* and *F* are now free to be started.

The current state of the scheduling of the activities is as follows.

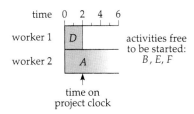

STEP 1 There are now three activities which may be started — activities *B*, *E* and *F*. Activity *E* has the smallest latest starting time, so we assign activity *E* to worker 1.

STEP 2 Advance the project clock to 5 minutes.

Activity *E* is completed, so worker 1 is free.

Activity *C* is now free to be started.

The current state of the scheduling of the activities is as follows.

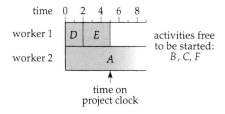

STEP 1 Of the three activities *B*, *C* and *F* which are free to be started, *B* and *C* are the most critical. Both have a latest starting time of 5 minutes.

We assign activity *C* to worker 1. (We have chosen *C* as it on the critical path, but *B* could have been chosen instead.)

STEP 2 Advance the project clock to 7 minutes.

Activity *A* is completed, so worker 2 is free.

No further activity is made free to be started by the completion of activity *A*.

STEP 1 Activities *B* and *F* are free to be started. Since activity *B* has the smaller latest starting time, we assign activity *B* to worker 2.

STEP 2 Advance the project clock to 12 minutes.

Activity *C* is completed, so worker 1 is free.

No further activity is made free to be started by the completion of activity *C*.

STEP 1 Activity *F* is the only activity which is free to be started, so we assign activity *F* to worker 1.

The current state of the scheduling of the activities is as follows.

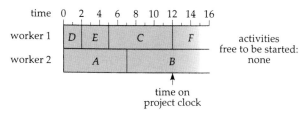

Since the project clock is now at 5 minutes, and since we cannot assign both activities *B* and *C* to workers at this point, there will be a delay in the completion of the project — in other words, the time taken with this schedule will be greater than the length of the critical path.

STEP 2 Advance the project clock to 14 minutes.

Activities B and F are completed, so both workers are free.

Activities G and J are now free to be started.

STEP 1 Activity J has the smaller latest starting time, so we assign activity J to worker 1.

The only remaining activity which can be started is G, so we assign activity G to worker 2.

STEP 2 Advance the project clock to 16 minutes.

Activity G is completed, so worker 2 is free.

Activities H and I are now free to be started.

STEP 1 Activities H and I have the same latest starting time. We assign activity H to worker 2.

STEP 2 Advance the project clock to 24 minutes.

Activity H is completed and worker 2 is free.

STEP 1 Activity I is the only remaining activity, so we assign activity I to worker 2.

STEP 2 Advance the project clock to 32 minutes.

All activities have now been completed and both workers are free. STOP.

The resulting schedule is the following.

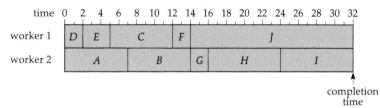

The schedule is the same as the one we obtained by trial and error. In other words, the algorithm produces an optimum schedule in this case. ∎

Problem 4.1

Use the critical path scheduling algorithm to schedule the building construction project for two workers. Do you obtain an optimum schedule?

The activity network, and the latest starting times and durations (in days) are as follows.

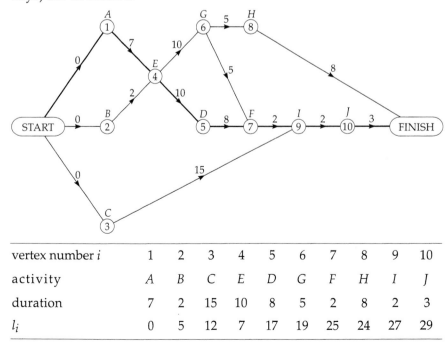

vertex number i	1	2	3	4	5	6	7	8	9	10
activity	A	B	C	E	D	G	F	H	I	J
duration	7	2	15	10	8	5	2	8	2	3
l_i	0	5	12	7	17	19	25	24	27	29

In the previous problem, and in the example discussed earlier, the critical path scheduling algorithm produces optimum schedules. In the next problem we consider a case in which the algorithm does not produce an optimum schedule.

Problem 4.2 ─────────────────────────────────

(a) For the project represented by the following activity network, find the critical path(s) and the latest starting times by inspection. The durations of the activities are in minutes.

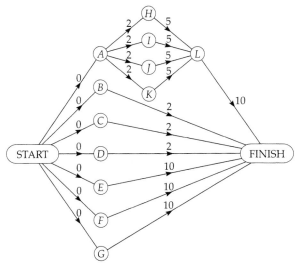

In this example, the vertices are numbered in alphabetical order, so we have omitted the numbers.

(b) Use the critical path scheduling algorithm to schedule this project for four workers. Do you obtain an optimum schedule?

───

4.2 Algorithms with protection schemes

In Problem 4.2 we obtained the following schedule.

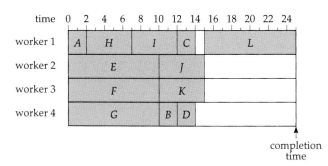

This schedule is far from an optimum one, as can be seen by comparing it with an optimum schedule such as the following.

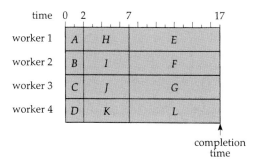

In a situation like this, it is obviously desirable to produce a schedule which has a shorter completion time than the one obtained by applying the algorithm. To do this in industry, some form of *protection scheme* is usually incorporated into an algorithm. There is no general protection scheme, so a network analyst working in a particular situation must develop a protection scheme which is appropriate for the type of scheduling problem involved. For example, for the project discussed in the above problem, a protection scheme may be incorporated in the algorithm as follows.

Outline of algorithm incorporating a protection scheme for the above example

STEP 1   Compute for each activity the sum of the earliest starting time and the latest starting time, and rank the activities in ascending order according to the values of these sums.

STEP 2   Assign activities successively to free workers according to this ranking, taking into account the precedence relations. If a preceding activity has not already been assigned, break the ranking order when assigning the activities.

This difficulty does not arise in our example.

We find the value of the sum of the earliest and latest starting times for each activity, and rank the activities according to the values of these sums as shown in the following table.

sum $e_i + l_i$	0	4	4	4	4	7	7	7	14	15	15	15
activity i	A	H	I	J	K	E	F	G	L	B	C	D
duration	2	5	5	5	5	10	10	10	10	2	2	2

We now go to Step 2, and assign each activity in turn to a free worker. If an activity cannot be assigned immediately because of the precedence relations, we wait until the appropriate previously assigned activities have been completed.

This procedure produces the following schedule.

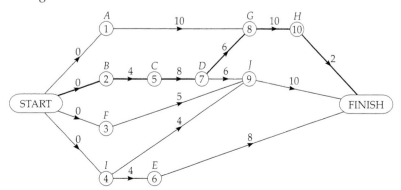

This is close to an optimum schedule. This schedule does not satisfy factory rule 1, but it comes close to satisfying factory rule 3.

Once we have produced a schedule using such a protection scheme, we may be able to improve it by moving activities to fill idle time intervals. For example, in the above schedule, it is a simple matter to fill the initial idle time intervals of workers 2, 3 and 4 with activities B, C and D. In this way we arrive at the optimum schedule we gave earlier.

Problem 4.3 ───────────────────────────

A project consists of ten activities A–J. The activity network and critical path are given below.

These were constructed in Problem 3.7.

42

The duration of each activity, and the earliest and latest starting times (in days) are as follows.

activity i	A	B	C	D	E	F	G	H	I	J
duration	10	4	8	6	8	5	10	2	4	10
e_i		0	0	4	12	4	0	18	28	0	18
l_i		8	0	4	12	22	15	18	28	16	20

(a) Apply the critical path scheduling algorithm to this project, given that two workers are available.

(b) Apply the modified scheduling algorithm incorporating a protection scheme to this project, given that two workers are available.

After studying this section, you should be able to:

- explain the terms *factory rules* and *protection scheme*;

- use the critical path scheduling algorithm to schedule activities for a number of workers, and the modified scheduling algorithm incorporating a protection scheme.

5 Bin packing

In the previous section we discussed scheduling problems in which we wish to schedule the activities of a project for a given number of workers so that the project is completed in the shortest possible time. We now turn the problem around, and ask for the minimum number of workers required to complete the project within a given period (which must, of course, be greater than or equal to the length of a critical path in the activity network for the project).

Suppose, for example, that a project consists of eleven activities A–K with the following durations (in days). There are no precedence relations.

activity	A	B	C	D	E	F	G	H	I	J	K
duration	8	8	2	9	6	9	5	4	6	9	7

What is the minimum number of workers required to finish the project in 15 days?

This problem is called a **bin-packing problem**, since it amounts to trying to pack the activities into the minimum number of 'bins' $b_1, b_2, ...,$ each of the specified capacity (in this case, 15 days).

There is no known algorithm which will always give an optimum solution to the bin-packing problem. However, there are a number of simple heuristic algorithms which usually give near optimum solutions.

One method is *next-fit packing*, in which the items (in this case, activities) are packed in the order in which they occur. The items are packed according to the following rule.

The order of occurrence is often given in a table, as above.

Next-fit packing algorithm

Always place the next item to be packed in the current bin if possible; otherwise, place it in the next bin.

If we pack the activities using the next-fit algorithm, we obtain the following packing.

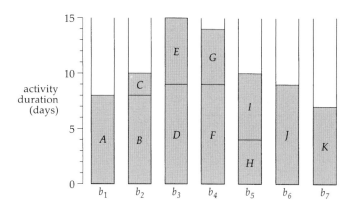

This packing scheme uses 7 bins so, in terms of our original problem, this scheme uses 7 workers to complete the project in 15 days.

Clearly, this algorithm is not very good because once a bin cannot accommodate a particular item that bin is never used again, even though a smaller item which *could* fit into it may appear later in the list. However, for *any* problem, this simple algorithm uses no more than twice the number of bins actually required.

To see this, suppose that n is the minimum number of bins needed according to the next-fit algorithm, and that each bin has capacity k. Let $c(b_i)$ denote the content of bin b_i packed according to the next-fit algorithm. The content of two successive bins b_i and b_{i+1} must be greater than k, otherwise bin b_{i+1} would not have been used. So we have

$$c(b_i) + c(b_{i+1}) > k, \qquad \text{for } i = 1, \ldots, n-1.$$

Thus, if n is even,

$$[c(b_1) + c(b_2)] + \cdots + [c(b_{n-1}) + c(b_n)] > \tfrac{1}{2} n \times k.$$

Since each bin has capacity k, an optimum packing needs at least $\tfrac{1}{2}n + 1$ bins.

And, if n is odd,

$$[c(b_1) + c(b_2)] + \cdots + [c(b_{n-2}) + c(b_{n-1})] + c(b_n) > \tfrac{1}{2}(n-1) \times k + c(b_n)$$

$$> \tfrac{1}{2}(n-1) \times k$$

Since each bin has capacity k, an optimum packing needs at least $\tfrac{1}{2}(n-1) \times k$ bins $= \tfrac{1}{2}n + \tfrac{1}{2}$ bins.

Thus the next-fit packing with n bins uses at most twice the optimum number of bins.

A better method is *first-fit packing*, in which the items are packed according to the following rule.

The upper bounds quoted in this section are *theoretical* bounds; in practice, the algorithms give much better results in many cases.

First-fit packing algorithm

Always place the next item to be packed in the lowest numbered bin which can accommodate that item.

It can be shown that the number of bins used in first-fit packing is at most 17/10 times the optimum number of bins.

If we pack the activities given above according to the first-fit packing algorithm, we obtain the packing shown at the top of page 45.

This packing uses only 6 bins, so it gives a better solution to our particular problem.

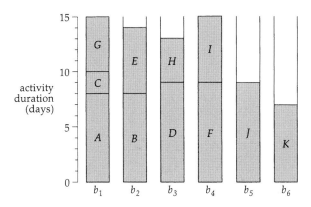

Notice that, in each of the above packings, the sum of the unfilled capacities of all the bins except the last is greater than the duration of activity K packed in the last bin. We might suspect that there is a better packing scheme which uses only 5 bins, but we have no means of finding out whether such a scheme exists, apart from trying other packing methods.

How can we improve on the first-fit method? Intuitively, it seems better to pack the activities with the longest durations first, so that we can use activities with smaller durations to fill the spaces in the bins already partially occupied. This idea is the basis of the *first-fit decreasing algorithm*, in which we fill the bins according to the following method.

First-fit decreasing packing algorithm

Order the items in decreasing order of size, and apply the first-fit packing procedure to this reordered list.

It can be shown that the number of bins used in first-fit decreasing packing is at most 11/9 times the optimum number of bins.

Let us apply this algorithm to our example.

First, we reorder the activities in decreasing order of duration (in days) as follows.

activity	D	F	J	A	B	K	E	I	G	H	C
duration	9	9	9	8	8	7	6	6	5	4	2

When we apply the first-fit algorithm, we obtain the following scheme.

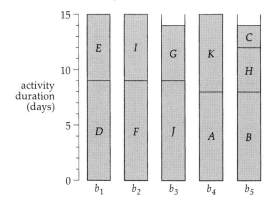

This packing scheme uses only 5 bins, so this problem requires the use of only 5 workers to complete the project within the given time period.

In this case, the first-fit decreasing algorithm has produced an optimum packing (that is, one using the fewest possible bins), but it does not produce an optimum packing in general. However, the first-fit decreasing algorithm is better than the first-fit algorithm, in the sense that it usually produces a packing with fewer bins.

The bin-packing problem occurs in many different practical situations, such as the following.

Example 5.1

A factory worker needs to pack items of various sizes into boxes as they come off a production line in no particular order. ■

Example 5.2

A plumber wishes to minimize the number of pipes of a standard length needed in order to cut a given number of lengths of pipe. In this case, the 'bins' are the standard length pipes, and the problem is to 'pack' the required lengths of pipe into the smallest number of the standard length pipes. ■

Example 5.3

A commercial television company which broadcasts with standard length breaks between programmes wishes to allocate advertisements. In this case, the 'bins' are the breaks between programmes, and the problem is to 'pack' advertisements into the smallest possible number of such breaks. ■

In Example 5.1, the items are available only one at a time, so no reordering of items is possible. In this situation, an algorithm such as the next-fit algorithm or the first-fit algorithm must be used. These algorithms are called **on-line algorithms**.

In Examples 5.2 and 5.3, it is possible to reorder the items to be packed, so the first-fit decreasing algorithm can be used. Such an algorithm involving reordering is called an **off-line algorithm**.

Problem 5.1

A carpenter has some planks of wood, each 12 feet long, and wishes to cut sections from these planks of the following lengths (in feet).

section	A	B	C	D	E	F	G	H	I	J	K	L
length	6	2	3	3	3	3	4	4	5	2	8	5

It is required to find a way of cutting these sections so that the minimum number of planks is used.

(a) Find a solution using the next-fit algorithm.

(b) Find a solution using the first-fit algorithm.

(c) Find a solution using the first-fit decreasing algorithm.

(d) By trial and error, find an optimum solution which uses fewer planks than the solutions obtained in parts (a), (b) and (c).

Problem 5.2

A project consists of eleven activities A–L with the following durations (in days).

activity	A	B	C	D	E	F	G	H	I	J	K	L
duration	6	2	6	2	6	2	6	2	6	2	6	2

It is required to find the minimum number of workers needed to complete the project in twelve days.

(a) Find a solution using the next-fit algorithm.

(b) Find a solution using the first-fit algorithm.

(c) Find a solution using the first-fit decreasing algorithm.

After studying this section, you should be able to:

- explain what is meant by the terms *bin-packing problem*, *on-line algorithm* and *off-line algorithm*;

- state and use the next-fit, first-fit, and the first-fit decreasing packing algorithms.

Further reading

Many of the topics discussed in Sections 1–4 are covered in:

V. Chachra, P. Ghare and J. Moore, *Applications of Graph Theory Algorithms*, Elsevier, 1979.

The above book also discusses many interesting applications of network theory.

A discussion of shortest path algorithms is given in:

N. Christofides, *Graph Theory: An Algorithmic Approach*, Academic Press, 1975.

T. C. Hu, *Combinatorial Algorithms*, Addison Wesley, 1982.

The latter also includes a discussion of bin-packing algorithms.

There are many excellent books on activity networks for project planning — in particular:

H. R. Hoare, *Project Management using Network Analysis*, McGraw-Hill, 1973;

K. G. Lockyer, *An Introduction to Critical Path Analysis*, Pitman Publishing Ltd, 1977;

A. Battersby, *Network Analysis for Planning and Scheduling*, 3rd edition, Macmillan, 1970.

Exercises

Section 1

1.1 Use the algorithm to find an Eulerian trail in the digraph D as in Worked problem 1.1, but when considering row 3 of the adjacency matrix, choose the non-zero entry a_{35}.

In the worked problem a_{31} was chosen.

1.2 The stored cycles in the solution to Problem 1.7 are:

$$C_1 = abda, \quad C_2 = acbea, \quad C_3 = cdec.$$

Find an Eulerian trail by using b as the vertex common to C_1 and C_2, and then e as the vertex common to the new C_1 and C_3.

1.3 Find all the Hamiltonian cycles in the digraph with the following adjacency matrix **A**.

$$\begin{array}{c} \\ a \\ b \\ c \\ d \end{array} \begin{array}{cccc} a & b & c & d \\ \begin{bmatrix} 0 & 1 & 0 & 0 \\ 0 & 0 & 1 & 1 \\ 1 & 0 & 0 & 0 \\ 1 & 0 & 1 & 0 \end{bmatrix} \end{array}$$

1.4 Find all the Hamiltonian cycles in the digraph with the following adjacency matrix **A**.

$$\begin{array}{c} \\ a \\ b \\ c \\ d \end{array} \begin{array}{cccc} a & b & c & d \\ \begin{bmatrix} 0 & 0 & 1 & 0 \\ 1 & 0 & 1 & 1 \\ 0 & 0 & 0 & 0 \\ 1 & 0 & 1 & 0 \end{bmatrix} \end{array}$$

Section 2

In each of the following exercises, you should use the appropriate algorithm. Solutions are given using the tabular method.

Shortest path algorithm

2.1 Find the shortest path from S to T and the shortest distance from S to each of the other vertices in the following weighted digraph.

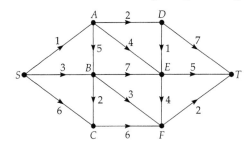

2.2 Find the shortest path(s) from S to T in the following weighted digraph.

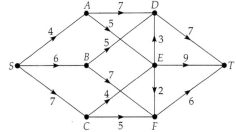

48

2.3 Find the shortest path(s) from S to T in the following weighted digraph.

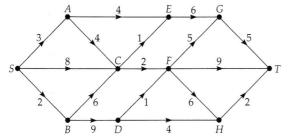

Longest path algorithm

2.4 Find the longest path from S to T and the longest distance from S to each of the other vertices in the weighted digraph of Exercise 2.1.

2.5 Find the longest path(s) from S to T in the weighted digraph of Exercise 2.2.

2.6 Find the longest path(s) from S to T in the following weighted digraph.

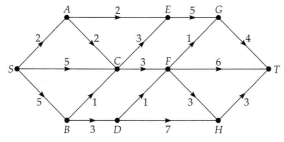

Section 3

Activity networks

All the exercises for this section refer to activity networks in which the vertices represent activities. Assume that there is no restriction on the number of workers available on a project.

3.1 Explain why the following network cannot be an activity network.

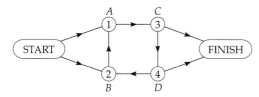

3.2 In the following activity network, two of the arcs are unnecessary. Which are they, and why can they be omitted?

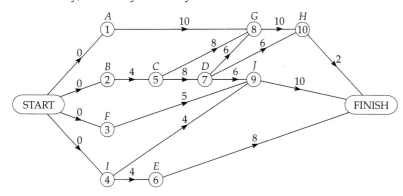

49

3.3 Suppose that you wish to redecorate a room and put in new self-assembly furniture. The activities to be carried out are as follows.

activity		duration (in hours)
C	lay carpet	6
W	lay wallpaper	10
P	paint woodwork	7
F	assemble furniture	3
H	hang curtains	2

(a) Construct a table of precedence relations for these activities.

(b) Draw an activity network and find the minimum completion time by inspection.

3.4 In the following activity network, the durations are in days.

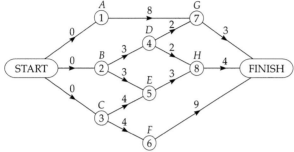

Find by inspection:

(a) the minimum completion time of the project;

(b) the earliest starting time of activity H;

(c) the latest starting time of activity H;

(d) the float for activity H.

Use of the algorithms

3.5 Suppose that the process of cooking breakfast is split up into the following activities with the given precedence relations.

activity		duration (in minutes)	preceding activities
A	grind coffee beans	1	
B	slice bread	2	
C	heat frying pan	3	
D	lay table	5	
E	make toast	3	B, C
F	make coffee	2	A
G	cook bacon	5	C
H	cook tomato	2	F, I
I	cook eggs	3	E, G

Using the algorithms:

(a) construct an activity network for this process;

(b) find a critical path and the minimum completion time;

(c) find the latest starting time and the float for each activity.

3.6 A project consists of eleven activities A–K. The duration of each activity and the activities that must precede each of them are as follows.

activity	duration (in days)	preceding activities
A	4	
B	5	A, E
C	5	
D	2	C, F
E	3	A, D
F	7	
G	2	E
H	6	D
I	2	B, G
J	3	F
K	3	H

Using the algorithms:

(a)   construct an activity network for this project;

(b)   find a critical path and the minimum completion time;

(c)   find the latest starting time and the float for each activity.

3.7 Suppose that in the activity network of Problem 3.5 we add an extra activity 4a of duration 5 days which must be completed after activity 3 and before activity 6, so that the activity network becomes as shown below.

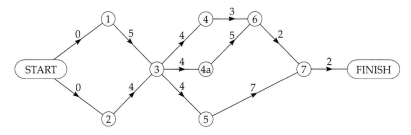

Find the critical path(s).

Section 4

Critical path scheduling algorithm

4.1 Apply the critical path scheduling algorithm to schedule the 11 jobs in the following activity network for two workers. There is only one critical path, which is indicated on the diagram. The latest starting times and durations (in days) for the activities are shown in the table below.

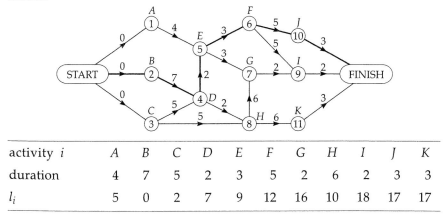

activity i	A	B	C	D	E	F	G	H	I	J	K
duration	4	7	5	2	3	5	2	6	2	3	3
l_i	5	0	2	7	9	12	16	10	18	17	17

4.2 For the project described in Exercise 4.1, how much time would be saved if three workers were available? Discuss the advantages and disadvantages of having three workers rather than two.

4.3 Apply the critical path scheduling algorithm to the activity network of Exercise 3.4 for two workers. There is only one critical path, which is indicated on the diagram. The latest starting times and durations (in days) for the activities are shown in the table below.

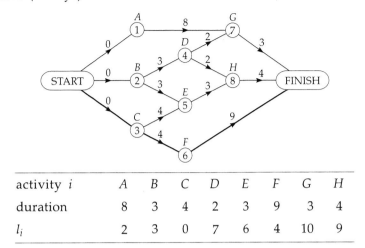

activity i	A	B	C	D	E	F	G	H
duration	8	3	4	2	3	9	3	4
l_i	2	3	0	7	6	4	10	9

Is your schedule an optimum schedule? If so, explain why; if not, find a better one.

4.4 In the following activity network, the durations are in days.

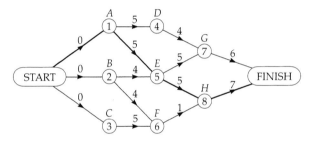

(a) What is the minimum completion time if an unlimited number of workers is available?

(b) What is the minimum completion time if only one worker is available?

(c) Use the critical path scheduling algorithm to schedule the project for two workers. The latest starting times and durations (in days) for the activities are shown in the table below.

activity i	A	B	C	D	E	F	G	H
duration	5	4	5	4	5	1	6	7
l_i	0	1	4	7	5	9	11	10

Is your schedule an optimum schedule?

4.5 Apply the critical path scheduling algorithm to the activity network for the process of cooking breakfast, obtained in Exercise 3.5, for each of the following cases. The activity network, and the latest starting times and durations (in days) for the activities are shown in the table on the facing page.

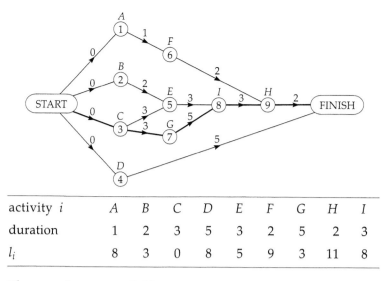

activity i	A	B	C	D	E	F	G	H	I
duration	1	2	3	5	3	2	5	2	3
l_i	8	3	0	8	5	9	3	11	8

(a) Three cooks are available.

(b) Two cooks are available.

In each case, determine whether your solution is an optimum schedule and, if not, find an optimum schedule.

Use of protection scheme

4.6 In Exercise 4.5(b) would it be advantageous to incorporate the protection scheme?

4.7 In the following activity network, the durations are in days. There is only one critical path, which is indicated on the diagram. The latest starting times and durations for the activities are shown in the table below.

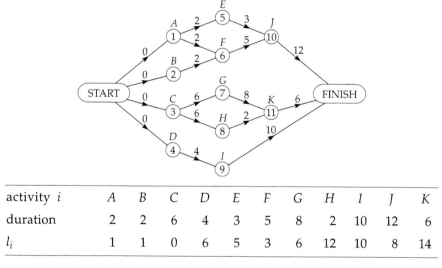

activity i	A	B	C	D	E	F	G	H	I	J	K
duration	2	2	6	4	3	5	8	2	10	12	6
l_i	1	1	0	6	5	3	6	12	10	8	14

(a) Schedule the activities for two workers, using the critical path scheduling algorithm.

(b) Find the earliest starting time for each activity, and hence schedule the activities for two workers, using the critical path scheduling algorithm with the protection scheme.

Section 5

5.1 Ten examinations (which must not overlap) are to be scheduled in the shortest possible number of days. The maximum allowable number of hours for examinations per day is 6, and the various examinations have the following durations (in hours).

examination	A	B	C	D	E	F	G	H	I	J
duration	1	3	4	1.5	2	3	1.5	3	1	4

(a) Find a solution using the next-fit algorithm.

(b) Find a solution using the first-fit algorithm.

(c) Find a solution using the first-fit decreasing algorithm.

(d) Find an optimum solution by trial and error.

5.2 A project consists of ten activities *A–J* with the following durations (in hours).

activity	A	B	C	D	E	F	G	H	I	J
duration	2	10	7	8	6	4	3	9	5	11

It is required to find the minimum number of workers needed to complete the project in 16 hours.

(a) Find a solution using the next-fit algorithm.

(b) Find a solution using the first-fit algorithm.

(c) Find a solution using the first-fit decreasing algorithm.

Solutions to the exercises

1.1 Using the algorithm, we take the following steps. (Here we use an abbreviated format and omit rows of zeros from the matrices.)

START   Set cycle counter $p = 0$.

$$\begin{array}{c c} & \begin{array}{c c c c c} a & b & c & d & e \end{array} \\ \begin{array}{c} a \\ b \\ c \\ d \\ e \end{array} & \begin{bmatrix} 0 & 1 & 0 & 0 & 0 \\ 0 & 0 & 1 & 0 & 0 \\ 1 & 0 & 0 & 0 & 1 \\ 0 & 0 & 1 & 0 & 0 \\ 0 & 0 & 0 & 1 & 0 \end{bmatrix} \end{array}$$

STEP 1   Set $p = 1$.

Row 1 has a non-zero entry, so $k = 1$.

Set $n = 1$, $C_1 = a\ldots$

$$\begin{array}{c c} & \begin{array}{c c c c c} a & b & c & d & e \end{array} \\ \begin{array}{c} b \\ c \\ d \\ e \end{array} & \begin{bmatrix} 0 & 0 & 1 & 0 & 0 \\ 1 & 0 & 0 & 0 & 1 \\ 0 & 0 & 1 & 0 & 0 \\ 0 & 0 & 0 & 1 & 0 \end{bmatrix} \end{array}$$

STEP 2 $a_{12} > 0$, so $m = 2$, $C_1 = ab\ldots$

Reduce a_{12} by 1 (to 0).

Set $n = 2$; $k = 1$, so $n \neq k$.

$$\begin{array}{c c} & \begin{array}{c c c c c} a & b & c & d & e \end{array} \\ \begin{array}{c} c \\ d \\ e \end{array} & \begin{bmatrix} 1 & 0 & 0 & 0 & 1 \\ 0 & 0 & 1 & 0 & 0 \\ 0 & 0 & 0 & 1 & 0 \end{bmatrix} \end{array}$$

STEP 2 $a_{23} > 0$, so $m = 3$, $C_1 = abc\ldots$

Reduce a_{23} by 1 (to 0).

Set $n = 3$; $k = 1$, so $n \neq k$.

$$\begin{array}{c c} & \begin{array}{c c c c c} a & b & c & d & e \end{array} \\ \begin{array}{c} c \\ d \\ e \end{array} & \begin{bmatrix} 1 & 0 & 0 & 0 & 0 \\ 0 & 0 & 1 & 0 & 0 \\ 0 & 0 & 0 & 1 & 0 \end{bmatrix} \end{array}$$

STEP 2 $a_{35} > 0$, so $m = 5$, $C_1 = abce\ldots$

Reduce a_{35} by 1 (to 0).

Set $n = 5$; $k = 1$, so $n \neq k$.

$$\begin{array}{c c} & \begin{array}{c c c c c} a & b & c & d & e \end{array} \\ \begin{array}{c} c \\ d \end{array} & \begin{bmatrix} 1 & 0 & 0 & 0 & 0 \\ 0 & 0 & 1 & 0 & 0 \end{bmatrix} \end{array}$$

STEP 2 $a_{54} > 0$, so $m = 4$, $C_1 = abced\ldots$

Reduce a_{54} by 1 (to 0).

Set $n = 4$; $k = 1$, so $n \neq k$.

$$\begin{array}{c c} & \begin{array}{c c c c c} a & b & c & d & e \end{array} \\ \begin{array}{c} c \end{array} & \begin{bmatrix} 1 & 0 & 0 & 0 & 0 \end{bmatrix} \end{array}$$

STEP 2 $a_{43} > 0$, so $m = 3$, $C_1 = abcedc\ldots$

Reduce a_{43} by 1 (to 0).

Set $n = 3$; $k = 1$, so $n \neq k$.

STEP 2 $a_{31} > 0$, so $m = 1$, $C_1 = abcedca$

Reduce a_{31} by 1 (to 0).

Set $n = 1$; $k = 1$, so $n = k$.

The matrix **A** has now been reduced to the zero matrix, so STORE $C_1 = abcedca$.

STEP 3   There is only one stored item, so this is the Eulerian trail:

   $abcedca$.

This is the trail we obtained in Worked problem 1.1.

1.2 In C_1 we replace b by C_2 (writing C_2 as $beacb$) to give $C_1 = abeacbda$. We delete C_2 from the store. The stored items are now

   $C_1 = abeacbda$ and $C_3 = cdec$.

In C_1 we replace e by C_3 (writing C_3 as $ecde$) to give $C_1 = abecdeacbda$. This is the required Eulerian trail.

1.3 The digraph has four vertices, so a Hamiltonian cycle has length 4, and $n = 4$.

STEP 1 The matrix **C** is as follows.

$$\mathbf{C} = \begin{bmatrix} 0 & ab & 0 & 0 \\ 0 & 0 & bc & bd \\ ca & 0 & 0 & 0 \\ da & 0 & dc & 0 \end{bmatrix}$$

Deleting the first vertex of each non-zero entry of **C**, we obtain

$$\mathbf{D} = \begin{bmatrix} 0 & b & 0 & 0 \\ 0 & 0 & c & d \\ a & 0 & 0 & 0 \\ a & 0 & c & 0 \end{bmatrix}$$

Set $k = 1$ and write $\mathbf{C}^1 = \mathbf{C}$.

STEP 2 We form $\mathbf{C}^2 = \mathbf{C}\ \#\ \mathbf{D}$.

$$\mathbf{C}^2 = \mathbf{C}\ \#\ \mathbf{D} = \begin{bmatrix} 0 & ab & 0 & 0 \\ 0 & 0 & bc & bd \\ ca & 0 & 0 & 0 \\ da & 0 & dc & 0 \end{bmatrix} \#\ \begin{bmatrix} 0 & b & 0 & 0 \\ 0 & 0 & c & d \\ a & 0 & 0 & 0 \\ a & 0 & c & 0 \end{bmatrix}$$

$$= \begin{bmatrix} 0 & 0 & abc & abd \\ \begin{matrix}bca\\bda\end{matrix} & 0 & bdc & 0 \\ 0 & cab & 0 & 0 \\ dca & dab & 0 & 0 \end{bmatrix}$$

STEP 3 Since $k + 1 = 2$ and $n = 4$, $k + 1 \neq n$, so set $k = 2$.

STEP 2 We form $\mathbf{C}^3 = \mathbf{C}^2\ \#\ \mathbf{D}$.

$$\mathbf{C}^3 = \mathbf{C}^2\ \#\ \mathbf{D} = \begin{bmatrix} 0 & 0 & abc & abd \\ \begin{matrix}bca\\bda\end{matrix} & 0 & bdc & 0 \\ 0 & cab & 0 & 0 \\ dca & dab & 0 & 0 \end{bmatrix} \#\ \begin{bmatrix} 0 & b & 0 & 0 \\ 0 & 0 & c & d \\ a & 0 & 0 & 0 \\ a & 0 & c & 0 \end{bmatrix}$$

$$= \begin{bmatrix} \begin{matrix}abca\\abda\end{matrix} & 0 & abdc & 0 \\ bdca & \begin{matrix}bcab\\bdab\end{matrix} & 0 & 0 \\ 0 & 0 & cabc & cabd \\ 0 & dcab & dabc & dabd \end{bmatrix}$$

STEP 3 Since $k + 1 = 3$ and $n = 4$, $k + 1 \neq n$, so set $k = 3$.

STEP 2 We form $\mathbf{C}^4 = \mathbf{C}^3\ \#\ \mathbf{D}$.

$$\mathbf{C}^4 = \mathbf{C}^3\ \#\ \mathbf{D} = \begin{bmatrix} \begin{matrix}abca\\abda\end{matrix} & 0 & abdc & 0 \\ bdca & \begin{matrix}bcab\\bdab\end{matrix} & 0 & 0 \\ 0 & 0 & cabc & cabd \\ 0 & dcab & dabc & dabd \end{bmatrix} \#\ \begin{bmatrix} 0 & b & 0 & 0 \\ 0 & 0 & c & d \\ a & 0 & 0 & 0 \\ a & 0 & c & 0 \end{bmatrix}$$

$$= \begin{bmatrix} abdca & 0 & 0 & 0 \\ 0 & bdcab & 0 & 0 \\ 0 & 0 & cabdc & 0 \\ 0 & 0 & 0 & dcabd \end{bmatrix}$$

STEP 3 Since $k + 1 = 4 = n$, STOP.

The entries in $\mathbf{C}^4$ are all the same, so there is only one Hamiltonian cycle, $abdca$.

1.4 The digraph has four vertices, so a Hamiltonian cycle has length 4, and $n = 4$.

STEP 1   The matrix $\mathbf{C}$ is as follows.

$$\mathbf{C} = \begin{bmatrix} 0 & 0 & ac & 0 \\ ba & 0 & bc & bd \\ 0 & 0 & 0 & 0 \\ da & 0 & dc & 0 \end{bmatrix}$$

Deleting the first vertex of each non-zero entry of $\mathbf{C}$, we obtain

$$\mathbf{D} = \begin{bmatrix} 0 & 0 & c & 0 \\ a & 0 & c & d \\ 0 & 0 & 0 & 0 \\ a & 0 & c & 0 \end{bmatrix}$$

Set $k = 1$ and write $\mathbf{C}^1 = \mathbf{C}$.

STEP 2   We form $\mathbf{C}^2 = \mathbf{C} \# \mathbf{D}$.

$$\mathbf{C}^2 = \mathbf{C} \# \mathbf{D} = \begin{bmatrix} 0 & 0 & ac & 0 \\ ba & 0 & bc & bd \\ 0 & 0 & 0 & 0 \\ da & 0 & dc & 0 \end{bmatrix} \# \begin{bmatrix} 0 & 0 & c & 0 \\ a & 0 & c & d \\ 0 & 0 & 0 & 0 \\ a & 0 & c & 0 \end{bmatrix}$$

$$= \begin{bmatrix} 0 & 0 & 0 & 0 \\ bda & 0 & \begin{matrix} bac \\ bdc \end{matrix} & 0 \\ 0 & 0 & 0 & 0 \\ 0 & 0 & dac & 0 \end{bmatrix}$$

STEP 3   Since $k + 1 = 2$ and $n = 4$, $k + 1 \neq n$, so set $k = 2$.

STEP 2   We form $\mathbf{C}^3 = \mathbf{C}^2 \# \mathbf{D}$.

$$\mathbf{C}^3 = \mathbf{C}^2 \# \mathbf{D} = \begin{bmatrix} 0 & 0 & 0 & 0 \\ bda & 0 & \begin{matrix} bac \\ bdc \end{matrix} & 0 \\ 0 & 0 & 0 & 0 \\ 0 & 0 & dac & 0 \end{bmatrix} \# \begin{bmatrix} 0 & 0 & c & 0 \\ a & 0 & c & d \\ 0 & 0 & 0 & 0 \\ a & 0 & c & 0 \end{bmatrix}$$

$$= \begin{bmatrix} 0 & 0 & bdac & 0 \\ 0 & 0 & 0 & 0 \\ 0 & 0 & 0 & 0 \\ 0 & 0 & 0 & 0 \end{bmatrix}$$

STEP 3   Since $k + 1 = 3$ and $n = 4$, $k + 1 \neq n$, so set $k = 3$.

STEP 2   We form $\mathbf{C}^4 = \mathbf{C}^3 \# \mathbf{D}$.

$$\mathbf{C}^4 = \mathbf{C}^3 \# \mathbf{D} = \begin{bmatrix} 0 & 0 & bdac & 0 \\ 0 & 0 & 0 & 0 \\ 0 & 0 & 0 & 0 \\ 0 & 0 & 0 & 0 \end{bmatrix} \# \begin{bmatrix} 0 & 0 & c & 0 \\ a & 0 & c & d \\ 0 & 0 & 0 & 0 \\ a & 0 & c & 0 \end{bmatrix}$$

$$= \begin{bmatrix} 0 & 0 & 0 & 0 \\ 0 & 0 & 0 & 0 \\ 0 & 0 & 0 & 0 \\ 0 & 0 & 0 & 0 \end{bmatrix}$$

STEP 3   Since $k + 1 = 4 = n$, STOP.

Thus there are no Hamiltonian cycles. Indeed, in this particular case, we can deduce this immediately from the adjacency matrix $\mathbf{A}$, since the third row tells us that there is no arc out of c.

2.1 We start by giving S zero potential.

iteration	origin vertex	vertices assigned labels						
		A	B	C	D	E	F	T
1	S	[1]	3	6				
2	A		[3]		[3]	5		
3	B			5			6	
	D					[4]		10
4	E			[5]				9
5	C						[6]	
6	F							[8]

Tracing back from T, we find the shortest path $SBFT$ with length 8.

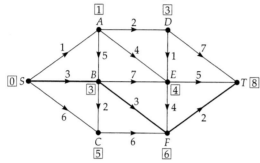

The required shortest distances are the potentials, as follows.

vertex	A	B	C	D	E	F	T
distance from S	1	3	5	3	4	6	8

2.2 We start by giving S zero potential.

iteration	origin vertex	vertices assigned labels						
		A	B	C	D	E	F	T
1	S	[4]	6	7				
2	A		[6]		11	9		
3	B			[7]	11		13	
4	C					[9]	12	
5	E				[11]		[11]	18
6	D							18
	F							[17]

Tracing back from T, we find the shortest path $SAEFT$ with length 17.

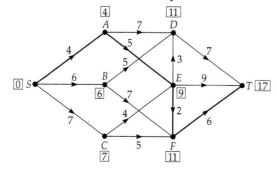

2.3 We start by giving S zero potential.

iteration	origin vertex	A	B	C	D	E	F	G	H	T
1	S	3	[2]	8						
2	B	[3]		8	11					
3	A			[7]		[7]				
4	C						[9]			
	E							13		
5	F				[11]				15	18
6	D						[13]		15	
7	G								[15]	18
8	H									[17]

Tracing back from T, we find two shortest paths $SBDHT$ and $SACFHT$ with length 17.

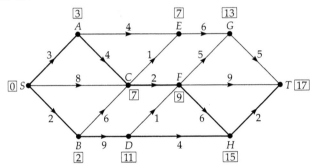

2.4 We start by giving S zero potential.

iteration	vertices assigned labels	S	A	B	C	D	E	F		vertex	distance from S
1 (S)	A	[1]								A	1
2 (S, A)	B	3	[6]							B	6
3 (S, A, B)	C	6		[8]						C	8
	D			[3]						D	3
4 (S, A, B, C, D)	E		5	[13]						E	13
5 (S, A, B, C, D, E)	F			9	14		[17]			F	17
6 (S, A, B, C, D, E, F)	T				10		18	[19]		T	19

Tracing back from T, we find the longest path $SABEFT$ with length 19.

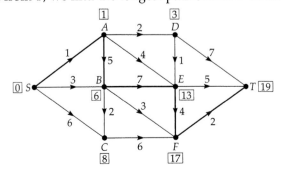

The required longest distances are the potentials, shown in the margin.

2.5 We start by giving S zero potential.

iteration	vertices assigned labels	origin vertices						
		S	A	B	C	D	E	F
1 (S)	A	[4]						
	B	[6]						
	C	[7]						
2 (S, A, B, C)	E		9		[11]			
3 (S, A, B, C, E)	D		11	11			[14]	
	F			[13]			[13]	
4 (S, A, B, C, D, E, F)	T					[21]		

Tracing back from T, we find the longest path $SCEDT$ with length 21.

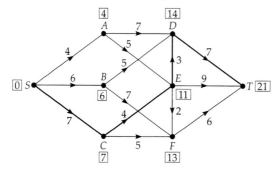

2.6 We start by giving S zero potential.

iteration	vertices assigned labels	origin vertices								
		S	A	B	C	D	E	F	G	H
1 (S)	A	[2]								
	B	[5]								
2 (S, A, B)	C	5	4	[6]						
	D			[8]						
3 (S, A, B, C, D)	E		4		[9]					
	F				[9]	[9]				
4 (S, A, B, C, D, E, F)	G						[14]	10		
	H					[15]		12		
5 (S, A, B, C, D, E, F, G, H)	T							15	[18]	[18]

Tracing back from T, we find two longest paths $SBCEGT$ and $SBDHT$ with length 18.

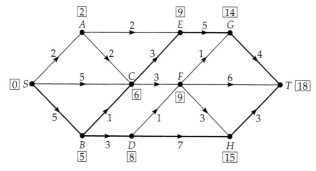

3.1 The given network cannot be an activity network, since it contains a cycle *ACDBA* and there are no weights on the arcs.

3.2 The arcs *CG* and *DH* are redundant, since they tell us that *C* must be completed before *G* (which we know from the arcs *CD* and *DG*), and that *D* must be completed before *H* (which we know from the arcs *DG* and *DH*).

3.3

(a) This example demonstrates that producing a table of precedence relations is not always straightforward. It may be necessary to make decisions about what the activities involve. In this example, activity *H* must be carried out after activities *W* and *P*, and it is probably desirable for *P* to precede *W*, and for *W* and *P* to precede *C*. We assume that the furniture is to be assembled in the same room, so activity *F* should probably come after activities *C*, *W* and *P*. (However, if the furniture is to be assembled in another room, then this could be done at any time.) With the above assumptions, we obtain the following precedence relations.

> *P* must precede *W*
>
> *W* must precede *H* and *C*
>
> *C* must precede *F*

(b) The activity network is shown below. The critical path is via vertices *P, W, C* and *F*, so the minimum completion time is $7 + 10 + 6 + 3 = 26$ hours.

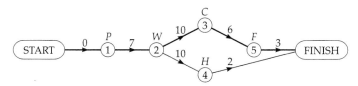

3.4

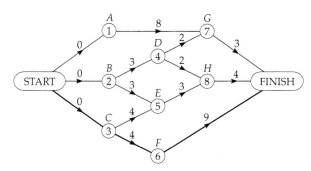

(a) The critical path is via vertices *C* and *F*, so the minimum completion time is $4 + 9 = 13$ days.

(b) The earliest starting time of activity *H* is the length of the longest path to *H*, that is, $4 + 3 = 7$ days.

(c) The latest starting time of activity *H* is

> (minimum completion time) – (duration of *H*) = $13 - 4 = 9$ days.

(d) The float for activity *H* is $9 - 7 = 2$ days.

3.5

(a) To start Part A of the algorithm for constructing an activity network, we draw a bipartite graph representing the precedence relations (shown on the left below). Applying Part A, we number the vertices as follows.

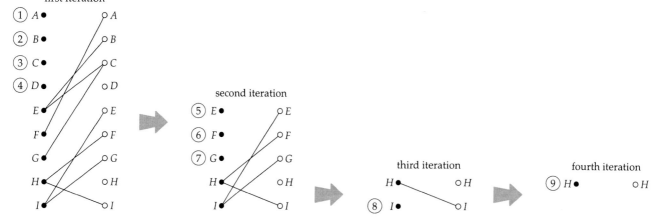

Applying Part B of the algorithm, we obtain the following activity network. We have also marked the critical path obtained in part (b).

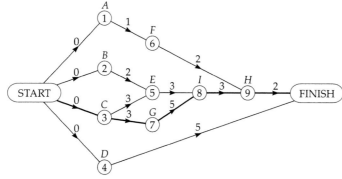

(b) Applying Part A of the critical path construction algorithm, we obtain the vertex labels shown in the following table. We have traced the critical path found in Part B of the algorithm.

j	i	e_i	$c_{i,j}$	$e_i + c_{i,j}$	e_j	p_j	activity numbered j
0	–	–	–	–	0	**0**	START
1	0	0	0	0	0	0	A
2	0	0	0	0	0	0	B
3	**0**	0	**0**	0	0	**0**	C
4	0	0	0	0	0	0	D
5	2	0	2	2			
5	3	0	3	3	3	3	E
6	1	0	1	1	1	1	F
7	**3**	0	**3**	3	3	**3**	G
8	5	3	3	6			
8	**7**	3	**5**	8	8	**7**	I
9	6	1	2	3			
9	**8**	8	3	11	11	**8**	H
10	4	0	5	5			
10	**9**	11	**2**	13	13	**9**	FINISH

The critical path is via vertices C, G, I and H. The length of the critical path is $0 + 3 + 5 + 3 + 2 = 13$, the value of e_{10}; thus the minimum completion time is 13 minutes.

(c) Applying the algorithm for finding the latest starting times, we obtain the following table.

i	j	l_j	$c_{i,j}$	$l_j - c_{i,j}$	l_i
10	–	–	–	–	13
9	10	13	2	11	11
8	9	11	3	8	8
7	8	8	5	3	3
6	9	11	2	9	9
5	8	8	3	5	5
4	10	13	5	8	8
3	5	5	3	2	
3	7	3	3	0	0
2	5	5	2	3	3
1	6	9	1	8	8
0	1	8	0	8	
0	2	3	0	3	
0	3	0	0	0	0
0	4	8	0	8	

The earliest and latest starting times and the floats are given in the following table.

activity numbered i	vertex number i	earliest starting time e_i	latest starting time l_i	float $l_i - e_i$
START	0	0	0	0
A	1	0	8	8
B	2	0	3	3
C	3	0	0	0
D	4	0	8	8
E	5	3	5	2
F	6	1	9	8
G	7	3	3	0
H	9	11	11	0
I	8	8	8	0
FINISH	10	13	13	0

3.6

(a) To start Part A of the algorithm for constructing an activity network, we draw a bipartite graph representing the precedence relations (shown on the left below).

Applying Part A of the algorithm, we number the vertices as follows.

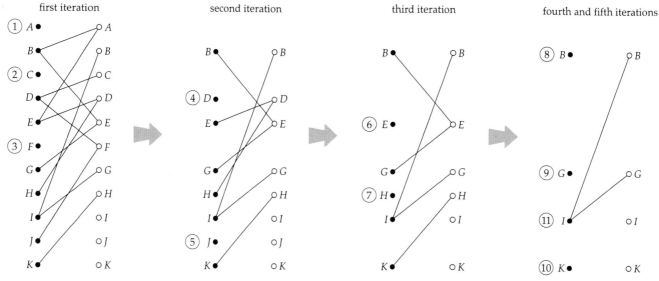

Applying Part B of the algorithm, we obtain the following activity network. We have also marked the critical path obtained in part (b) below.

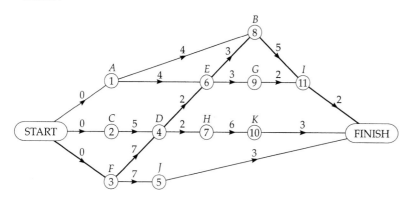

(b) Applying Part A of the critical path construction algorithm, we obtain the following table. We have traced the critical path found in Part B of the algorithm.

j	i	e_i	$c_{i,j}$	$e_i + c_{i,j}$	e_j	p_j	activity numbered j
0	–	–	–	–	0	**0**	START
1	0	0	0	0	0	0	A
2	0	0	0	0	0	0	C
3	**0**	0	**0**	0	0	**0**	F
4	2	0	5	5			
4	**3**	0	7	7	7	**3**	D
5	3	0	7	7	7	3	J
6	1	0	4	4			
6	**4**	7	2	9	9	**4**	E
7	4	7	2	9	9	4	H
8	1	0	4	4			
8	**6**	9	3	12	12	**6**	B
9	6	9	3	12	12	6	G
10	7	9	6	15	15	7	K
11	**8**	12	5	17	17	**8**	I
11	9	12	2	14			
12	**11**	17	2	19	19	**11**	FINISH
12	10	15	3	18			
12	5	7	3	10			

The critical path is via vertices F, D, E, B and I. The length of the critical path is $0 + 7 + 2 + 3 + 5 + 2 = 19$, the value of e_{12}; thus the minimum completion time is 19 days.

(c) Applying the algorithm for finding the latest starting times, we obtain the following table.

i	j	l_j	$c_{i,j}$	$l_j - c_{i,j}$	l_i
12	–	–	–	–	19
11	12	19	2	17	17
10	12	19	3	16	16
9	11	17	2	15	15
8	11	17	5	12	12
7	10	16	6	10	10
6	8	12	3	9	9
6	9	15	3	12	
5	12	19	3	16	16
4	6	9	2	7	7
4	7	10	2	8	
3	4	7	7	0	0
3	5	16	7	9	
2	4	7	5	2	2
1	6	9	4	5	
1	8	12	4	8	8
0	1	8	0	8	
0	2	2	0	2	
0	3	0	0	0	0

The earliest and latest starting times and the floats are given in the following table.

activity numbered i	vertex number i	earliest starting time e_i	latest starting time l_i	float $l_i - e_i$
START	0	0	0	0
A	1	0	8	8
C	2	0	2	2
F	3	0	0	0
D	4	7	7	0
J	5	7	16	9
E	6	9	9	0
H	7	9	10	1
B	8	12	12	0
G	9	12	15	3
K	10	15	16	1
I	11	17	17	0
FINISH	12	19	19	0

3.7 Applying the critical path construction algorithm, we obtain the following table.

j	i	e_i	$c_{i,j}$	$e_i + c_{i,j}$	e_j	p_j
0	–	–	–	–	0	**0**
1	0	0	0	0	0	0
2	0	0	0	0	0	0
3	**1**	0	5	5	5	**1**
3	2	0	4	4		
4	3	5	4	9	9	3
4a	**3**	5	4	9	9	**3**
5	**3**	5	4	9	9	**3**
6	4	9	3	12		
6	**4a**	9	5	14	14	**4a**
7	**6**	14	2	16	16	**6**
7	**5**	9	7	16	16	**5**
8	**7**	16	2	18	18	**7**

The addition of the extra activity now gives two critical paths: via activities 1, 3, 5 and 7; and via activities 1, 3, 4a, 6 and 7.

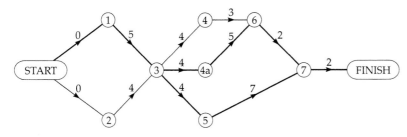

4.1 Applying the critical path scheduling algorithm, we obtain the following schedule requiring 22 days.

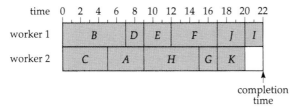

4.2 With three workers it is possible to save just two hours. The critical path scheduling algorithm gives the following schedule requiring 20 days.

If the total time for the project must be kept to an absolute minimum and money is available for a third worker, then it may be justifiable to employ three workers for the project. Note that if three workers are used, then the precedence relations force at least one worker to be idle much of the time. To avoid this, worker 3 could be brought in just for the days needed, and employed on other projects on the other days. On the other hand, if money is short and taking two extra days is acceptable, then it may be better to use just two workers.

4.3 We obtain the following schedule requiring 19 days for two workers.

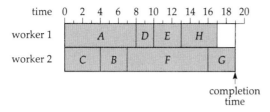

This is not an optimum solution. An optimum solution requiring 18 days is as follows.

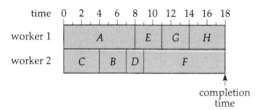

4.4

(a) The critical path is via vertices A, E and H. The minimum completion time is therefore $0 + 5 + 5 + 7 = 17$ days if an unlimited number of workers is available.

(b) If only one worker is available, the minimum completion time is the sum of the durations of the activities: $5 + 4 + 5 + 4 + 5 + 1 + 6 + 7 = 37$ days.

(c) We obtain the following schedule requiring 19 days for two workers.

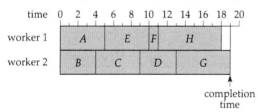

This is an optimum schedule as the only idle time is the one day that worker 1 finishes ahead of worker 2 and there is no way of avoiding this.

4.5

(a) Applying the critical path scheduling algorithm, we obtain the following schedule requiring 13 minutes.

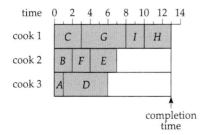

This is an optimum schedule, since the time taken (13 minutes) does not exceed the length of the critical path through vertices C, G, I and H.

(b) Applying the critical path scheduling algorithm, we obtain the following schedule requiring 15 minutes.

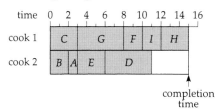

This is not an optimum schedule. An optimum schedule requiring 13 minutes is as follows.

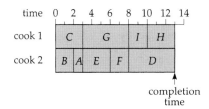

4.6 We add the earliest and latest starting times for each activity, and rank the activities according to the values of these sums as follows.

sum $e_i + l_i$	0	3	6	8	8	8	10	16	22
activity i	C	B	G	A	D	E	F	I	H
duration	3	2	5	1	5	3	2	3	2

If we now apply the critical path scheduling algorithm with the activities with sum 8 taken in the order A, E, D, we obtain the same schedule as in Exercise 4.5(b) requiring 15 minutes.

Taking the activities with sum 8 in the order A, D, E, we obtain the following schedule requiring 16 minutes.

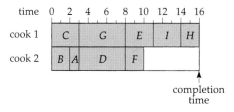

Taking the activities with sum 8 in the order D, A, E, we obtain the following schedule requiring 16 minutes.

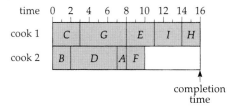

Taking the activities with sum 8 in the order D, E, A, we obtain the following schedule requiring 15 minutes.

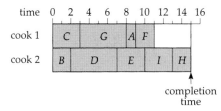

Thus there is no advantage in using the protection scheme for this example.

The algorithm does not permit us to schedule activity E before activity A or activity D.

69

4.7

(a) We obtain the following schedule requiring 33 days for two workers.

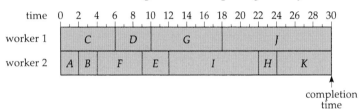

(b) The earliest and latest starting times, and the sum of these two times for each activity are given below. The activities are ranked according to the values of these sums.

activity i	C	A	B	F	D	E	G	I	J	H	K
l_i	0	1	1	3	6	5	6	10	8	12	14
e_i	0	0	0	2	0	2	6	4	7	6	14
$e_i + l_i$	0	1	1	5	6	7	12	14	15	18	28
duration	6	2	2	5	4	3	8	10	12	2	6

We obtain the following schedule requiring 30 days for two workers.

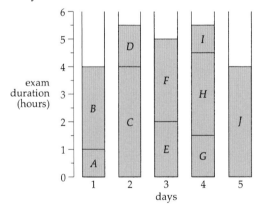

5.1

(a) Using the next-fit algorithm, we obtain the following schedule requiring 5 days.

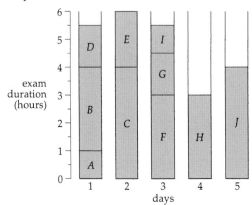

(b) Using the first-fit algorithm, we obtain the following schedule requiring 5 days.

(c)   Using the first-fit decreasing algorithm, we again obtain a schedule
      requiring 5 days. In this schedule, only one hour of day 5 is used and
      half an hour is unused on each of days 2 and 4.

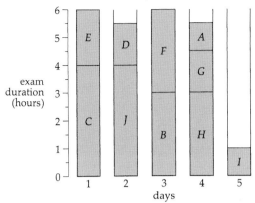

(d)   By trial and error, we obtain the following optimum schedule
      requiring only 4 days.

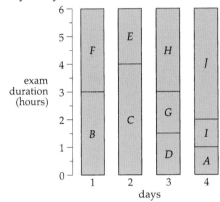

Other optimum schedules can be
obtained by interchanging activities
of the same duration, for example, B,
F and H.

5.2

(a)   Using the next-fit algorithm, we obtain the following schedule
      requiring 5 workers.

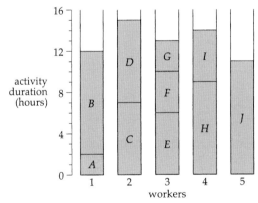

(b)   Using the first-fit algorithm, we obtain the following schedule
      requiring 5 workers.

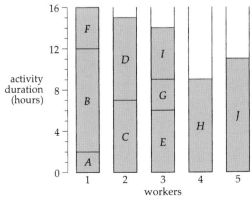

(c) Using the first-fit decreasing algorithm, we obtain the following schedule requiring 5 workers.

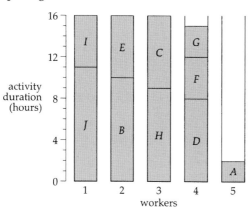

The total completion time is 65 hours, so the project cannot be completed in 16 hours with fewer than 5 workers.

Solutions to the problems

Solution 1.1

(a)

	a	b	c	d
a	0	2	1	0
b	0	0	0	1
c	1	0	0	0
d	2	1	0	0

	a	b	c	d
a	2	1	0	0
b	0	2	1	0
c	0	0	0	1
d	1	0	0	2

numbers of walks of length 2   numbers of walks of length 3

(b)

$$\mathbf{A}^2 = \begin{bmatrix} 0 & 2 & 1 & 0 \\ 0 & 0 & 0 & 1 \\ 1 & 0 & 0 & 0 \\ 2 & 1 & 0 & 0 \end{bmatrix} \qquad \mathbf{A}^3 = \begin{bmatrix} 2 & 1 & 0 & 0 \\ 0 & 2 & 1 & 0 \\ 0 & 0 & 0 & 1 \\ 1 & 0 & 0 & 2 \end{bmatrix}$$

(c)   The tables in part (a) correspond to the matrix products in part (b). For example, the number of walks of length 2 from d to a is the entry in row 4 (corresponding to d) and column 1 (corresponding to a) in the matrix $\mathbf{A}^2$; a similar result holds for the numbers of walks of length 3 and the entries in $\mathbf{A}^3$.

Solution 1.2

$$\mathbf{A} = \begin{bmatrix} 0 & 1 & 0 & 0 & 1 \\ 1 & 0 & 1 & 0 & 0 \\ 0 & 0 & 0 & 2 & 0 \\ 0 & 0 & 0 & 0 & 1 \\ 0 & 0 & 1 & 1 & 0 \end{bmatrix} \qquad \mathbf{A}^2 = \begin{bmatrix} 1 & 0 & 2 & 1 & 0 \\ 0 & 1 & 0 & 2 & 1 \\ 0 & 0 & 0 & 0 & 2 \\ 0 & 0 & 1 & 1 & 0 \\ 0 & 0 & 0 & 2 & 1 \end{bmatrix}$$

$$\mathbf{A}^3 = \begin{bmatrix} 0 & 1 & 0 & 4 & 2 \\ 1 & 0 & 2 & 1 & 2 \\ 0 & 0 & 2 & 2 & 0 \\ 0 & 0 & 0 & 2 & 1 \\ 0 & 0 & 1 & 1 & 2 \end{bmatrix} \qquad \mathbf{A}^4 = \begin{bmatrix} 1 & 0 & 3 & 2 & 4 \\ 0 & 1 & 2 & 6 & 2 \\ 0 & 0 & 0 & 4 & 2 \\ 0 & 0 & 1 & 1 & 2 \\ 0 & 0 & 2 & 4 & 1 \end{bmatrix}$$

The numbers of walks from b to d of lengths 1, 2, 3 and 4 are given by the entries in row 2 column 4 of the matrices $\mathbf{A}$, $\mathbf{A}^2$, $\mathbf{A}^3$ and $\mathbf{A}^4$, respectively — namely, 0, 2, 1 and 6.

There is no walk of length 1, 2, 3 or 4 from d to b, since each of the matrices $\mathbf{A}$, $\mathbf{A}^2$, $\mathbf{A}^3$ and $\mathbf{A}^4$ has 0 in row 4 column 2.

Solution 1.3

$$\mathbf{B} = \mathbf{A} + \mathbf{A}^2 + \mathbf{A}^3 + \mathbf{A}^4 = \begin{bmatrix} 2 & 2 & 5 & 7 & 7 \\ 2 & 2 & 5 & 9 & 5 \\ 0 & 0 & 2 & 8 & 4 \\ 0 & 0 & 2 & 4 & 4 \\ 0 & 0 & 4 & 8 & 4 \end{bmatrix}$$

The matrix $\mathbf{B}$ contains some non-diagonal entries which are zero, so the digraph is not strongly connected, by Theorem 1.2.

Note that this fact was already clear from the last part of Solution 1.2, so in this case it was not necessary to calculate $\mathbf{B}$ explicitly.

Solution 1.4

The adjacency matrix $\mathbf{A}$ is a 5×5 matrix, so the digraph has five vertices. We therefore need to find $\mathbf{A}$, $\mathbf{A}^2$, $\mathbf{A}^3$, $\mathbf{A}^4$ and $\mathbf{B} = \mathbf{A} + \mathbf{A}^2 + \mathbf{A}^3 + \mathbf{A}^4$.

The digraph with adjacency matrix $\mathbf{A}$ is

$$\mathbf{A} = \begin{bmatrix} 0 & 0 & 0 & 1 & 0 \\ 1 & 0 & 1 & 0 & 0 \\ 0 & 0 & 0 & 1 & 0 \\ 0 & 0 & 0 & 0 & 1 \\ 0 & 1 & 0 & 0 & 0 \end{bmatrix} \quad \mathbf{A}^2 = \begin{bmatrix} 0 & 0 & 0 & 0 & 1 \\ 0 & 0 & 0 & 2 & 0 \\ 0 & 0 & 0 & 0 & 1 \\ 0 & 1 & 0 & 0 & 0 \\ 1 & 0 & 1 & 0 & 0 \end{bmatrix}$$

which you met in *Graphs 1*, Problem 3.12(b).

$$\mathbf{A}^3 = \begin{bmatrix} 0 & 1 & 0 & 0 & 0 \\ 0 & 0 & 0 & 0 & 2 \\ 0 & 1 & 0 & 0 & 0 \\ 1 & 0 & 1 & 0 & 0 \\ 0 & 0 & 0 & 2 & 0 \end{bmatrix} \quad \mathbf{A}^4 = \begin{bmatrix} 1 & 0 & 1 & 0 & 0 \\ 0 & 2 & 0 & 0 & 0 \\ 1 & 0 & 1 & 0 & 0 \\ 0 & 0 & 0 & 2 & 0 \\ 0 & 0 & 0 & 0 & 2 \end{bmatrix}$$

$$\mathbf{B} = \begin{bmatrix} 1 & 1 & 1 & 1 & 1 \\ 1 & 2 & 1 & 2 & 2 \\ 1 & 1 & 1 & 1 & 1 \\ 1 & 1 & 1 & 2 & 1 \\ 1 & 1 & 1 & 2 & 2 \end{bmatrix}$$

Each non-diagonal entry in $\mathbf{B}$ is positive, so the digraph with adjacency matrix $\mathbf{A}$ is strongly connected, by Theorem 1.2.

Solution 1.5

(a) The adjacency matrix $\mathbf{A}$ is given below.

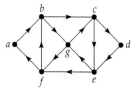

$$\begin{array}{c|ccccccc} & a & b & c & d & e & f & g \\ \hline a & 0 & 1 & 0 & 0 & 0 & 0 & 0 \\ b & 0 & 0 & 1 & 0 & 0 & 0 & 1 \\ c & 0 & 0 & 0 & 1 & 1 & 0 & 0 \\ d & 0 & 0 & 0 & 0 & 1 & 0 & 0 \\ e & 0 & 0 & 0 & 0 & 0 & 1 & 1 \\ f & 1 & 1 & 0 & 0 & 0 & 0 & 0 \\ g & 0 & 0 & 1 & 0 & 0 & 1 & 0 \end{array}$$

outdeg a = indeg a = 1
outdeg b = indeg b = 2
outdeg c = indeg c = 2
outdeg d = indeg d = 1
outdeg e = indeg e = 2
outdeg f = indeg f = 2
outdeg g = indeg g = 2

(b) For each vertex,

> the sum of the entries in the corresponding *row* of $\mathbf{A}$
> = the *out-degree* of the vertex

and

> the sum of the entries in the corresponding *column* of $\mathbf{A}$
> = the *in-degree* of the vertex.

Solution 1.6

outdeg a = 1 = indeg a

outdeg b = 1 = indeg b

outdeg c = 2 = indeg c

outdeg d = 1 = indeg d

outdeg e = 1 = indeg e

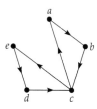

It follows from Theorem 1.3 that the digraph is Eulerian. (We can see that the digraph is connected by inspection of $\mathbf{A}$.)

From the adjacency matrix, we obtain the digraph shown above.

An Eulerian trail is *abcedca*.

Solution 1.7

	matrix	cycle number p	label at start and end of cycle k	vertex k v_k	current label in cycle n	column of A m	vertex m v_m	cycle
START	$\begin{array}{c|ccccc} & a & b & c & d & e \\ \hline a & 0 & 1 & 1 & 0 & 0 \\ b & 0 & 0 & 0 & 1 & 1 \\ c & 0 & 1 & 0 & 1 & 0 \\ d & 1 & 0 & 0 & 0 & 1 \\ e & 1 & 0 & 1 & 0 & 0 \end{array}$	0						
STEP 1	Row 1 has a non-zero entry.	1	1	$v_1 = a$	1			$C_1 = a\ldots$
STEP 2	Choose $a_{12} > 0$. Reduce a_{12} by 1 (to 0). $n \neq k$.	1	1		2	2	$v_2 = b$	$C_1 = ab\ldots$
STEP 2	Choose $a_{24} > 0$. Reduce a_{24} by 1 (to 0). $n \neq k$.	1	1		4	4	$v_4 = d$	$C_1 = abd\ldots$
STEP 2	Choose $a_{41} > 0$. Reduce a_{41} by 1 (to 0). $n = k$. Not all elements of A are zero.	1	1		1	1	$v_1 = a$	$C_1 = abda$
								STORE C_1
STEP 1	$\begin{array}{c|ccccc} & a & b & c & d & e \\ \hline a & 0 & 0 & 1 & 0 & 0 \\ b & 0 & 0 & 0 & 0 & 1 \\ c & 0 & 1 & 0 & 1 & 0 \\ d & 0 & 0 & 0 & 0 & 1 \\ e & 1 & 0 & 1 & 0 & 0 \end{array}$							
	Row 1 has a non-zero entry.	2	1	$v_1 = a$	1			$C_2 = a\ldots$
STEP 2	$a_{13} = 1$. Reduce a_{13} by 1 (to 0). $n \neq k$.	2	1		3	3	$v_3 = c$	$C_2 = ac\ldots$
STEP 2	Choose $a_{32} = 1$. Reduce a_{32} by 1 (to 0). $n \neq k$.	2	1		2	2	$v_2 = b$	$C_2 = acb\ldots$
STEP 2	$a_{25} = 1$. Reduce a_{25} by 1 (to 0). $n \neq k$.	2	1		5	5	$v_5 = e$	$C_2 = acbe\ldots$
STEP 2	Choose $a_{51} = 1$. Reduce a_{51} by 1 (to 0). $n = k$. Not all elements of A are zero.	2	1		1	1	$v_1 = a$	$C_2 = acbea$
								STORE C_2

(continued overleaf)

	matrix	cycle number p	label at start and end of cycle k	vertex k v_k	current label in cycle n	column of **A** m	vertex m v_m	cycle
STEP 1	$\begin{array}{c} \quad a\ b\ c\ d\ e \\ a \\ b \\ c \\ d \\ e \end{array}\begin{bmatrix} 0 & 0 & 0 & 0 & 0 \\ 0 & 0 & 0 & 0 & 0 \\ 0 & 0 & 0 & 1 & 0 \\ 0 & 0 & 0 & 0 & 1 \\ 0 & 0 & 1 & 0 & 0 \end{bmatrix}$							
	Row 3 has a non-zero entry.	3	3	$v_3 = c$	3			$C_3 = c...$
STEP 2	$a_{34} = 1.$ Reduce a_{34} by 1 (to 0). $n \neq k.$	3	3		4	4	$v_4 = d$	$C_3 = cd...$
STEP 2	$a_{45} = 1.$ Reduce a_{45} by 1 (to 0). $n \neq k.$	3	3		5	5	$v_5 = e$	$C_3 = cde...$
STEP 2	$a_{53} = 1.$ Reduce a_{53} by 1 (to 0). $n = k.$	3	3		3	3	$v_3 = c$	$C_3 = cdec$
	All elements of **A** have now been reduced to zero.							STORE C_3

STEP 3   The stored cycles are $C_1 = abda$, $C_2 = acbea$ and $C_3 = cdec$.

C_1 and C_2 have vertex a in common.

In C_1 replace one a by C_2 to give $C_1 = abdacbea$.

Delete C_2 from the store.

The stored items are now $C_1 = abdacbea$ and $C_3 = cdec$. (Note that C_1 is no longer a cycle.)

C_1 and C_3 have vertex c in common.

In C_1 replace c by C_3 to give $C_1 = abdacdecbea$.

C_1 is now an Eulerian trail $abdacdecbea$.

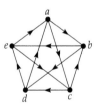

Solution 1.8

$$C^2 = C \# D = \begin{bmatrix} 0 & ab & 0 & ad \\ 0 & 0 & bc & bd \\ ca & 0 & 0 & 0 \\ 0 & 0 & dc & 0 \end{bmatrix} \# \begin{bmatrix} 0 & b & 0 & d \\ 0 & 0 & c & d \\ a & 0 & 0 & 0 \\ 0 & 0 & c & 0 \end{bmatrix} = \begin{bmatrix} 0 & 0 & \genfrac{}{}{0pt}{}{abc}{adc} & abd \\ bca & 0 & bdc & 0 \\ 0 & cab & 0 & cad \\ dca & 0 & 0 & 0 \end{bmatrix}$$

$$C^3 = C^2 \# D = \begin{bmatrix} 0 & 0 & \genfrac{}{}{0pt}{}{abc}{adc} & abd \\ bca & 0 & bdc & 0 \\ 0 & cab & 0 & cad \\ dca & 0 & 0 & 0 \end{bmatrix} \# \begin{bmatrix} 0 & b & 0 & d \\ 0 & 0 & c & d \\ a & 0 & 0 & 0 \\ 0 & 0 & c & 0 \end{bmatrix} = \begin{bmatrix} \genfrac{}{}{0pt}{}{abca}{adca} & 0 & abdc & 0 \\ bdca & bcab & 0 & bcad \\ 0 & 0 & \genfrac{}{}{0pt}{}{cabc}{cadc} & cabd \\ 0 & dcab & 0 & dcad \end{bmatrix}$$

$$C^4 = C^3 \# D = \begin{bmatrix} \genfrac{}{}{0pt}{}{abca}{adca} & 0 & abdc & 0 \\ bdca & bcab & 0 & bcad \\ 0 & 0 & \genfrac{}{}{0pt}{}{cabc}{cadc} & cabd \\ 0 & dcab & 0 & dcad \end{bmatrix} \# \begin{bmatrix} 0 & b & 0 & d \\ 0 & 0 & c & d \\ a & 0 & 0 & 0 \\ 0 & 0 & c & 0 \end{bmatrix} = \begin{bmatrix} abdca & 0 & 0 & 0 \\ 0 & bdcab & 0 & 0 \\ 0 & 0 & cabdc & 0 \\ 0 & 0 & 0 & dcabd \end{bmatrix}$$

Solution 1.9

STEP 1   The matrix $\mathbf{C}$ is as follows.

$$\mathbf{C} = \begin{bmatrix} 0 & ab & 0 & ad \\ ba & 0 & 0 & bd \\ ca & cb & 0 & 0 \\ 0 & 0 & dc & 0 \end{bmatrix}$$

Deleting the first vertex of each non-zero entry of $\mathbf{C}$, we obtain

$$\mathbf{D} = \begin{bmatrix} 0 & b & 0 & d \\ a & 0 & 0 & d \\ a & b & 0 & 0 \\ 0 & 0 & c & 0 \end{bmatrix}$$

Set $k = 1$ and write $\mathbf{C}^1 = \mathbf{C}$.

STEP 2   We form $\mathbf{C}^2 = \mathbf{C} \,\#\, \mathbf{D}$.

$$\mathbf{C}^2 = \begin{bmatrix} 0 & ab & 0 & ad \\ ba & 0 & 0 & bd \\ ca & cb & 0 & 0 \\ 0 & 0 & dc & 0 \end{bmatrix} \# \begin{bmatrix} 0 & b & 0 & d \\ a & 0 & 0 & d \\ a & b & 0 & 0 \\ 0 & 0 & c & 0 \end{bmatrix} = \begin{bmatrix} aba & 0 & adc & abd \\ 0 & bab & bdc & bad \\ cba & cab & 0 & \begin{matrix} cad \\ cbd \end{matrix} \\ dca & dcb & 0 & 0 \end{bmatrix}$$

STEP 3   Since $k + 1 = 2$ and $n = 4$, $k + 1 \neq n$, so set $k = 2$.

STEP 2   We form $\mathbf{C}^3 = \mathbf{C}^2 \,\#\, \mathbf{D}$.

$$\mathbf{C}^3 = \begin{bmatrix} aba & 0 & adc & abd \\ 0 & bab & bdc & bad \\ cba & cab & 0 & \begin{matrix} cad \\ cbd \end{matrix} \\ dca & dcb & 0 & 0 \end{bmatrix} \# \begin{bmatrix} 0 & b & 0 & d \\ a & 0 & 0 & d \\ a & b & 0 & 0 \\ 0 & 0 & c & 0 \end{bmatrix} = \begin{bmatrix} adca & adcb & abdc & 0 \\ bdca & bdcb & badc & 0 \\ 0 & 0 & \begin{matrix} cadc \\ cbdc \end{matrix} & \begin{matrix} cbad \\ cabd \end{matrix} \\ dcba & dcab & 0 & \begin{matrix} dcad \\ dcbd \end{matrix} \end{bmatrix}$$

STEP 3   Since $k + 1 = 3$ and $n = 4$, $k + 1 \neq n$, so set $k = 3$.

STEP 2   We form $\mathbf{C}^4 = \mathbf{C}^3 \,\#\, \mathbf{D}$.

$$\mathbf{C}^4 = \begin{bmatrix} adca & adcb & abdc & 0 \\ bdca & bdcb & badc & 0 \\ 0 & 0 & \begin{matrix} cadc \\ cbdc \end{matrix} & \begin{matrix} cbad \\ cabd \end{matrix} \\ dcba & dcab & 0 & \begin{matrix} dcad \\ dcbd \end{matrix} \end{bmatrix} \# \begin{bmatrix} 0 & b & 0 & d \\ a & 0 & 0 & d \\ a & b & 0 & 0 \\ 0 & 0 & c & 0 \end{bmatrix} = \begin{bmatrix} \begin{matrix} adcba \\ abdca \end{matrix} & 0 & 0 & 0 \\ 0 & \begin{matrix} bdcab \\ badcb \end{matrix} & 0 & 0 \\ 0 & 0 & \begin{matrix} cbadc \\ cabdc \end{matrix} & 0 \\ 0 & 0 & 0 & \begin{matrix} dcbad \\ dcabd \end{matrix} \end{bmatrix}$$

STEP 3   Since $k + 1 = 4 = n$, STOP.

The entries in $\mathbf{C}^4$ are the required Hamiltonian cycles
      $adcba$ and $abdca$.

Solution 3.1

Part A: procedure for numbering the vertices

We draw a bipartite graph representing the precedence relations, as shown below.

activity	preceding activities
J	A, B, C, D, E
C	D, E
E	D
F	D
H	E, F, G
I	E, F, G
G	F

The numbering of the vertices carried out in each successive iteration is shown in the following diagrams.

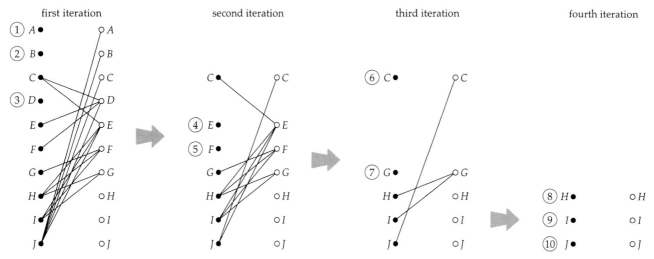

We now construct the activity network following the procedure of Part B of the algorithm. The resulting activity network is the following.

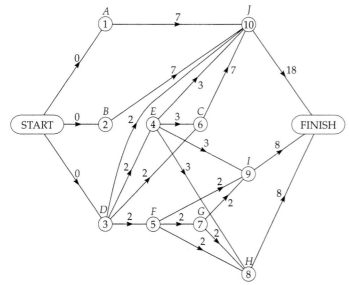

activity network for bicycle assembly

The details of the construction of this network are given on the facing page.

Part B: procedure for drawing the activity network

STEP 3   We draw the START vertex, and the vertices numbered in the first iteration: A, B and D. We then draw arcs from the START vertex to A, B and D, assigning a zero weight to each.

STEP 4   In the second iteration we numbered vertices E and F, so we add vertices E and F to the activity network.

Activity D must precede E and F, so we draw arcs:

from D to E, with weight 2 (the duration of D);
from D to F, with weight 2 (the duration of D).

STEP 4   In the third iteration we numbered vertices C and G , so we add vertices C and G to the activity network.

Activities D and E must precede C, and activity F must precede G, so we draw arcs:

from D to C, with weight 2 (the duration of D);
from E to C, with weight 3 (the duration of E);
from F to G, with weight 2 (the duration of F).

STEP 4   In the fourth iteration we numbered vertices H, I and J, so we add vertices H, I and J to the activity network.

Activities E, F and G must precede H and I, so we draw arcs:

from E to H and from E to I, with weight 3 (the duration of E);
from F to H and from F to I, with weight 2 (the duration of F);
from G to H and from G to I, with weight 2 (the duration of G).

Activities A, B, C, D and E must precede J, so we draw arcs:

from A to J, with weight 7 (the duration of A);
from B to J, with weight 7 (the duration of B);
from C to J, with weight 7 (the duration of C);
from D to J, with weight 2 (the duration of D);
from E to J, with weight 3 (the duration of E).

All the activities have now been represented by vertices in the activity network.

STEP 5   We draw a FINISH vertex. From the terminal vertices H, I and J, we draw arcs:

from H to FINISH, with weight 8 (the duration of H);
from I to FINISH, with weight 8 (the duration of I);
from J to FINISH, with weight 18 (the duration of J).

The activity network is now complete.

Solution 3.2

The arcs DJ and EJ are redundant, since activity J must follow activity C which must follow activity E which must follow activity D.

Similarly, the arc FI is redundant.

The redundant precedence relations are given in the following table.

activity	preceding activities
I	F
J	D, E
H	F
C	D

Solution 3.3

Let us imagine that we steadily increase the delay in completing an activity which is not on the critical path. To begin with, this delay will not affect the time needed to complete the project. However, as the delay increases, there will come a point when the delay becomes so large that the activity becomes part of a new critical path, so delays larger than this will delay the project.

Solution 3.4

Applying Part A of the critical path construction algorithm, we obtain the vertex labels shown in the following table.

The critical path is found using Part B, and is indicated on the table and in the activity network below.

j	i	e_i	$c_{i,j}$	$e_i + c_{i,j}$	e_j	p_j	activity numbered j
0	–	–	–	–	0	0	START
1	0	0	0	0	0	0	A
2	0	0	0	0	0	0	B
3	0	0	0	0	0	0	D
4	3	0	2	2	2	3	E
5	3	0	2	2	2	3	F
6	3	0	2	2			
6	4	2	3	5	5	4	C
7	5	2	2	4	4	5	G
8	4	2	3	5			
8	5	2	2	4			
8	7	4	2	6	6	7	H
9	4	2	3	5			
9	5	2	2	4			
9	7	4	2	6	6	7	I
10	1	0	7	7			
10	2	0	7	7			
10	3	0	2	2			
10	4	2	3	5			
10	6	5	7	12	12	6	J
11	8	6	8	14			
11	9	6	8	14			
11	10	12	18	30	30	10	FINISH

The critical path is via vertices D, E, C and J, as shown below.

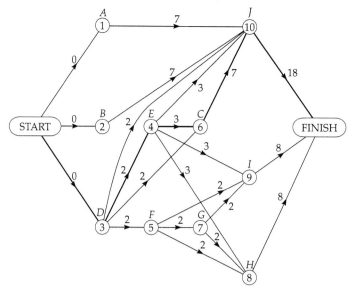

activity network for bicycle assembly

The length of the critical path is $0 + 2 + 3 + 7 + 18 = 30$, the value of e_{11}; thus the minimum completion time is 30 minutes.

Solution 3.5

(a) The minimum completion time is equal to the length of the critical path, which is

$$0 + 5 + 4 + 7 + 2 = 18 \text{ days.}$$

(b) The earliest starting time of activity 4 is equal to the length of the longest path from the START vertex to vertex 4. This longest path passes through vertices 1 and 3, and its length is $0 + 5 + 4 = 9$ days, so

$$e_4 = 9.$$

Activity 6 cannot start until activity 4 has been completed, and the duration of activity 4 is 3 days; thus the earliest starting time for activity 6 is $9 + 3 = 12$ days, so

$$e_6 = 12.$$

(c) We can find the latest starting time for activity 6 by working backwards from the FINISH vertex. The minimum completion time is 18 days, so activity 7 must begin after $18 - 2 = 16$ days, and hence activity 6 must begin at the latest after $16 - 2 = 14$ days, so

$$l_6 = 14.$$

Activity 4 must begin not later than 3 days before the latest starting time of activity 6; thus the latest starting time for activity 6 is $14 - 3 = 11$ days, so

$$l_4 = 11.$$

(d) The float of activity 4 is $l_4 - e_4 = 11 - 9 = 2$ days.

The float of activity 6 is $l_6 - e_6 = 14 - 12 = 2$ days.

(e) If activity 4 is delayed by 2 days, then the path through vertices 3, 4, 6 and 7 becomes part of a new critical path. So if activity 6 is also delayed by 2 days, this causes a delay of 2 days in the completion of the whole project. In other words, the two activities cannot both be delayed by their float times without delaying the whole project.

Solution 3.6

(a) Applying the algorithm for finding the latest starting times, we obtain the following table.

i	j	l_j	$c_{i,j}$	$l_j - c_{i,j}$	l_i
11	–	–	–	–	30
10	11	30	18	12	12
9	11	30	8	22	22
8	11	30	8	22	22
7	8	22	2	20	20
7	9	22	2	20	
6	10	12	7	5	5
5	7	20	2	18	18
5	8	22	2	20	
5	9	22	2	20	
4	6	5	3	2	2
4	8	22	3	19	
4	9	22	3	19	
4	10	12	3	9	
3	4	2	2	0	0
3	5	18	2	16	
3	6	5	2	3	
3	10	12	2	10	
2	10	12	7	5	5
1	10	12	7	5	5
0	1	5	0	5	
0	2	5	0	5	
0	3	0	0	0	0

(b) The earliest and latest starting times and the floats are given in the following table.

activity numbered i	vertex number i	earliest starting time e_i	latest starting time l_i	float $l_i - e_i$
START	0	0	0	0
A	1	0	5	5
B	2	0	5	5
D	3	0	0	0
E	4	2	2	0
F	5	2	18	16
C	6	5	5	0
G	7	4	20	16
H	8	6	22	16
I	9	6	22	16
J	10	12	12	0
FINISH	11	30	30	0

82

Solution 3.7

(a) The activity network is shown below.

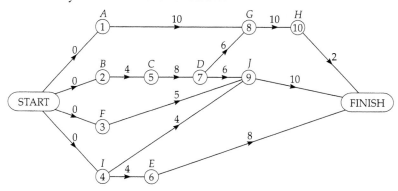

(b) Applying Part A of the critical path construction algorithm, we obtain the following table. We have traced the critical path found in Part B of the algorithm.

j	i	e_i	$c_{i,j}$	$e_i + c_{i,j}$	e_j	p_j	activity numbered j
0	–	–	–	–	0	0	**START**
1	0	0	0	0	0	0	A
2	**0**	0	**0**	0	0	**0**	B
3	0	0	0	0	0	0	F
4	0	0	0	0	0	0	I
5	**2**	0	**4**	4	4	**2**	C
6	4	0	4	4	4	4	E
7	**5**	4	**8**	12	12	**5**	D
8	1	0	10	10			
8	**7**	12	**6**	18	18	**7**	G
9	3	0	5	5			
9	4	0	4	4			
9	7	12	6	18	18	7	J
10	**8**	18	**10**	28	28	**8**	H
11	6	4	8	12			
11	9	18	10	28			
11	**10**	28	**2**	30	30	**10**	**FINISH**

The critical path is via vertices B, C, D, G and H. The length of the critical path is $0 + 4 + 8 + 6 + 10 + 2 = 30$, the value of e_{11}; thus the minimum completion time is 30 days.

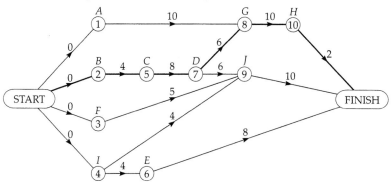

(c) Applying the algorithm for finding the latest starting times, we obtain the following table.

i	j	l_j	$c_{i,j}$	$l_j - c_{i,j}$	l_i
11	–	–	–	–	30
10	11	30	2	28	28
9	11	30	10	20	20
8	10	28	10	18	18
7	8	18	6	12	12
	9	20	6	14	
6	11	30	8	22	22
5	7	12	8	4	4
4	6	22	4	18	
	9	20	4	16	16
3	9	20	5	15	15
2	5	4	4	0	0
1	8	18	10	8	8
0	1	8	0	8	
0	2	0	0	0	0
0	3	15	0	15	
0	4	16	0	16	

The earliest and latest starting times and the floats are given in the following table.

activity numbered i	vertex number i	earliest starting time e_i	latest starting time l_i	float $l_i - e_i$
START	0	0	0	0
A	1	0	8	8
B	2	0	0	0
F	3	0	15	15
I	4	0	16	16
C	5	4	4	0
E	6	4	22	18
D	7	12	12	0
G	8	18	18	0
J	9	18	20	2
H	10	28	28	0
FINISH	11	30	30	0

Solution 4.1

The steps involved in applying the algorithm are given below.

START   Set project clock to 0 days.

STEP 1   Activity A is assigned to worker 1.
             Activity B is assigned to worker 2.

STEP 2   Advance project clock to 2 days.
             Activity B is completed; worker 2 is free.

STEP 1   Activity C is assigned to worker 2.

STEP 2   Advance project clock to 7 days.
             Activity A is completed; worker 1 is free.
             Activity E is free to be started.

STEP 1   Activity E is assigned to worker 1.

STEP 2   Advance project clock to 17 days.
             Activities C and E are completed; both workers are free.
             Activities D and G are free to be started.

STEP 1   Activity D is assigned to worker 1.
             Activity G is assigned to worker 2.

STEP 2   Advance project clock to 22 days.
             Activity G is completed; worker 2 is free.
             Activity H is free to be started.

STEP 1   Activity H is assigned to worker 2.

STEP 2   Advance project clock to 25 days.
             Activity D is completed; worker 1 is free.
             Activity F is free to be started.

The current state of the scheduling of activities is as follows.

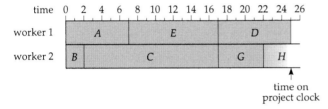

STEP 1   Activity F is assigned to worker 1.

STEP 2   Advance project clock to 27 days.
             Activity F is completed; worker 1 is free.
             Activity I is free to be started.

STEP 1   Activity I is assigned to worker 1.

STEP 2   Advance project clock to 29 days.
             Activity I is completed; worker 1 is free.
             Activity J is free to be started.

STEP 1   Activity J is assigned to worker 1.
             All the activities have been assigned.

STEP 2   Advance project clock to 30 days.
             Activity H is completed; worker 2 is free.

STEP 3   Advance project clock to 32 days.
             All the activities have been completed. STOP.

The final schedule is shown below. It is an optimum schedule — no other schedule has a shorter completion time.

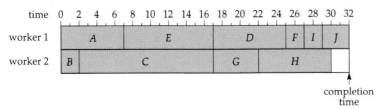

Solution 4.2

(a) By inspection, there are four critical paths via vertices A, H, L; A, I, L; A, J, L; A, K, L. The minimum completion time is 17 minutes.

The latest starting times and durations (in minutes) for the activities are given below.

activity i	A	B	C	D	E	F	G	H	I	J	K	L
duration	2	2	2	2	10	10	10	5	5	5	5	10
l_i	0	15	15	15	7	7	7	2	2	2	2	7

(b) Applying the critical path scheduling algorithm, we obtain the following schedule requiring 25 minutes for four workers.

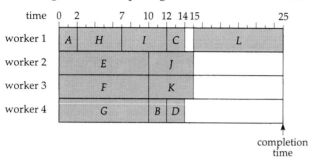

Solution 4.3

(a) Applying the critical path scheduling algorithm, we obtain the following schedule requiring 36 days for two workers.

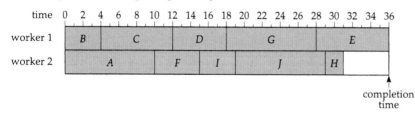

(b) We find the value of the sum of the earliest and latest starting times for each activity, and rank the activities according to the values of these sums, as shown in the following table.

sum $e_i + l_i$	0	8	8	15	16	24	26	36	38	56
activity i	B	A	C	F	I	D	E	G	J	H
duration	4	10	8	5	4	6	8	10	10	2

Applying the modified critical path scheduling algorithm with protection scheme, we obtain the following schedule requiring 34 days for two workers.

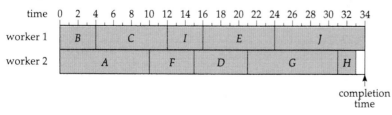

Solution 5.1

(a) Using the next-fit algorithm, we obtain the following plan requiring 6 planks.

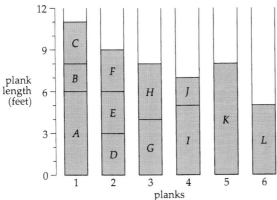

(b) Using the first-fit algorithm, we obtain the following plan requiring 5 planks.

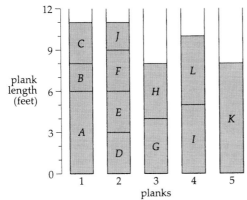

(c) Using the first-fit decreasing algorithm, we obtain the following plan requiring 5 planks; in this plan only two feet of plank 5 are used and one foot is unused in each of planks 2 and 4.

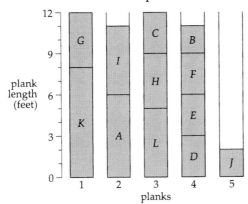

(d) By trial and error, we obtain the following optimum plan requiring only 4 planks.

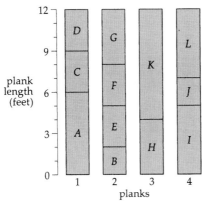

Other optimum plans can be obtained by interchanging sections of the same lengths.

Solution 5.2

(a) Using the next-fit algorithm, we obtain the following schedule requiring 6 workers.

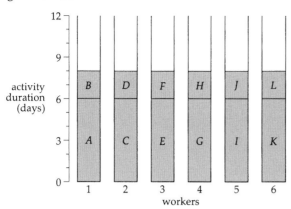

(b) Using the first-fit algorithm, we obtain the following schedule requiring 4 workers, which is clearly an optimum schedule.

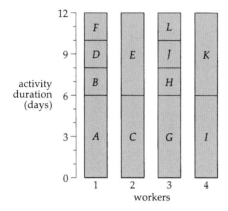

(c) Using the first-fit decreasing algorithm, we obtain the following schedule requiring 4 workers, which is clearly an optimum schedule.

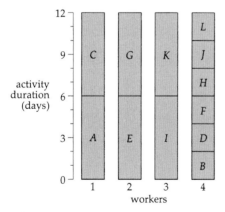

Index